104,50

108

87

94,95

119

156

122

127
Ored S.
129

108

P 48

admired
anemosites
of Lincoln

99

98

extensive
bibliography

107

22

149

commerc

# THE LITTLE GIANT

## Stephen A. Douglas

Born: April 23, 1813
Died: June 3, 1861

Stephen A. Douglas was considered by many of his contemporaries to be the greatest statesman of the period in which he lived. Diminutive in stature, a man of fiery speech and convictions, he was justly known as "The Little Giant" for the prowess he displayed in political battles. As a senator he championed all causes that would increase the prestige and size of the United States, including the growth of railroads, the war with Mexico, the Missouri Compromise. He supported popular sovereignty, arousing the wrath of both slaveholders and Abolitionists, and his series of debates with Abraham Lincoln left their mark on American history. When Lincoln defeated him in the presidential race of 1860, Douglas offered his services to his former adversary and fought for the preservation of the Union they both loved.

*Books by*

JEANNETTE COVERT NOLAN

ABRAHAM LINCOLN

ANDREW JACKSON

BENEDICT ARNOLD
Traitor to His Country

DOLLEY MADISON

FLORENCE NIGHTINGALE

THE GAY POET
The Story of Eugene Field

GEORGE ROGERS CLARK
Soldier and Hero

JOHN BROWN

LA SALLE AND THE GRAND ENTERPRISE

THE LITTLE GIANT
Stephen A. Douglas

O. HENRY
The Story of William Sydney Porter

THE SHOT HEARD ROUND THE WORLD
The Story of Lexington and Concord

SPY FOR THE CONFEDERACY
Rose O'Neal Greenhow

THE STORY OF CLARA BARTON OF THE RED CROSS

TREASON AT THE POINT

# THE LITTLE GIANT

## Stephen A. Douglas

by

### Jeannette Covert Nolan

13088

JULIAN MESSNER        NEW YORK

Published by Julian Messner
Division of Pocket Books, Inc.
8 West 40 Street, New York 10018

Third printing, 1965

921
Douglas

Sg  5-20-66  3.19

Printed in the United States of America

Library of Congress Catalog Card No. 64-11369

# CONTENTS

# AUTHOR'S NOTE

The surname of the subject of this book was originally and until 1845 spelled with the double "s"—Douglass; and it was so that Stephen Arnold Douglass was christened. But as he went into politics and before the electorate, he thought to simplify his name and dropped the final "s"; thus, history records him—Stephen Arnold Douglas.

Following the precedent of other biographers, I have throughout used the spelling that he himself preferred.

J. C. N.

# THE LITTLE GIANT

## Stephen A. Douglas

# 1

# SPRING, 1828

Stephen Douglas walked rapidly along the village street, mounted the front steps of the large brick house—and suddenly felt rather breathless. The April afternoon was unseasonably warm and he had been hurrying, a stack of books balanced under one arm and his woolen jacket buttoned snugly around his neck. For a moment he stared at the white-porticoed door and the imposing brass plate with its inscription: BRANDON ACADEMY, MR. J. N. CHIPMAN, SUPERINTENDENT. Then he squared his sturdy shoulders and resolutely rattled the knocker.

A maidservant, neat in gray skirts, starchy apron and bonnet, opened the door. "Yes?" she said.

Stephen pulled off his cap. "May I speak to the superintendent, please, if he's in and at leisure?"

The maid hesitated, glancing suspiciously at the books. "Have you some business with Mr. Chipman?"

"Yes, ma'am. Important business. At least," Stephen said, "important to me."

"You're not selling something? A book agent?"

"Oh, no! I'm just on my way home from school—the Brandon day school. It's the end of term, you know—"

"What's your name?"

He gave it in full: "Stephen Arnold Douglas. I think Mr.

11

Chipman may remember the name; it was my father's name, my father was a doctor."

"I'll inquire whether Mr. Chipman will see you," the maid said. "Wipe your boots clean on the mat and come in."

Murmuring his thanks, Stephen watched as she rustled down a wide hall, through a door at the rear. Presently she reappeared and beckoned him into a spacious library where a coal fire burned on the hearth and an elderly man, black-coated, with steel-rimmed spectacles astride his nose, was rising from behind a paper-strewn desk.

Stephen bowed politely. "Mr. Chipman?"

Mr. Chipman bowed also. "And you're Dr. Douglas' son, eh?"

"Yes, sir. I'm sorry to bother you."

"No bother. I was merely writing a few letters. Sit down." Mr. Chipman pushed forward a chair and seated himself again at the desk. "Of course, I remember your father—a prominent citizen of Brandon and as fine a physician as ever practiced in the state of Vermont! We were fortunate to have him here; the whole community grieved when he died so young and untimely. And you have business with me?"

Stephen sat down, his books on his lap. "I want to enroll as an academy pupil," he said. "I know your classes have adjourned for the summer vacation, but I thought you might give me a certificate of admission for next semester and I could be studying for the examinations. I've heard they're not easy."

Mr. Chipman smiled. "On the contrary, my examinations are as difficult as I can make them. Have you completed your work at the day school?"

"Yes, sir, only an hour ago. The master there said that you have more boys applying than you can accommodate. I do hope you'll accept me. I've brought my record card; it shows that my grades have been satisfactory."

Mr. Chipman read the card that Stephen handed to him. "Quite satisfactory." He added reflectively, "I believe you look like your father. The same black hair and blue eyes—yes, you're very like him. I recall that he died of a heart attack. How old were you then?"

"I was three months old, sir."

Mr. Chipman nodded. "I understand he was holding you at the time, and as he fell, he dropped you and your chin was deeply gashed by the sharp edge of the andirons. I see that you still bear the scar."

"Yes, sir." Stephen rubbed his chin which, though scarred, was firm and broad—an obstinate chin.

"Tragic," sighed Mr. Chipman. "Especially for your poor mother. I knew her slightly, as a girl. She was Sally Fisk then. You live now with her brother, Mr. Edward Fisk, on his farm, eh?"

"We live on the farm, but Mother is half owner of it," Stephen corrected quickly. "She and Uncle Edward inherited the property jointly from my Grandfather Fisk. Uncle Edward manages it, but we've never been dependent on him. Or on anybody else."

"I see. And how old are you now, Stephen?"

"I'll be fifteen in a couple of weeks." He waited for the comment that usually followed the mention of his age. When Mr. Chipman said nothing, he offered it himself. "Not very tall for fifteen, am I? An inch over five feet! I may grow a bit more, there's a chance I will. But maybe not. Oh, well! I'm healthy and strong, and height isn't everything. Napoleon wasn't tall, either."

"Napoleon?" Mr. Chipman echoed blankly, as if astonished at this turn in the conversation. "No, the French emperor was considerably below average in stature. But—why do you think of him?"

"Oh, I think of him a lot, sir. Not that I exactly admire him;

he's not a hero of mine, I wouldn't have him as a model—"

"Indeed, I trust not! Napoleon's ambition to conquer the world caused millions of innocent people to suffer."

"Yes. But I can understand why he was such a fighter," Stephen said earnestly. "When you're a little man, you've got to be scrappy or the bigger fellows will badger and bully you and trample you into the dust. At any rate, that's been my experience."

Mr. Chipman took a pinch of snuff from a silver box on his desk, removed his spectacles, polished them, placed them on his nose and peered at his visitor. "Your father was a graduate of Middlebury College. I presume you wish to study medicine, as he did?"

"No, sir. I'm interested in the law—and politics."

"Ah? Perhaps you dream of being President of the United States. It is the dream of every American boy."

Stephen grinned. "Well, I wouldn't mind tackling the job. But first I'd like to get elected to the Senate. Senator Douglas! And a ripsnorting Democrat! You see, sir, Andrew Jackson of Tennessee is really my hero."

"Andrew Jackson?" Mr. Chipman's astonishment seemed to increase; he took another pinch of snuff. "I dare say you know that Democrats are a rarity in our part of the country. I fear that as a politician of Senator Jackson's stripe you wouldn't progress fast or far in New England."

"Oh, I won't stay in New England, sir. I want to go out West where Democrats are plentiful."

"And does your mother agree to this?"

"Yes, Mother and I agree in everything. She thinks of education as an investment. She's interested in politics too, and we've had lawyers in the family on both the Fisk and the Douglas sides."

"You have discussed your plans with your uncle also?"

"Not *discussed*." Stephen paused. "Uncle Edward isn't a discussing sort of person. He's quiet, never says a word unless he has to. Some people in Brandon have the notion that he's stingy, tightfisted. Once a boy at school said, 'Your uncle is a skinflint miser!' I was mad as hops. I had to lick the rascal for it. Uncle Edward is *careful* about money; he'd rather save than spend it. But he's always been kind to me and to my sister Sarah, and fair with Mother in the farm dealings. And he knows my plans. He ought to, for he's listened often enough while Mother and I talked about them!"

"Without raising objections?"

"Not a single one, sir. Uncle Edward will be in favor of my entering the academy!"

Mr. Chipman extracted a slip of paper from his writing portfolio and lifted his quill pen. "I'm glad to have this good report of Mr. Fisk. He's a bachelor, I believe—"

"No," Stephen said. "He *was* a bachelor, until last spring when he surprised us by getting married. We're awfully fond of his wife. We all get along fine together. They're expecting a baby now."

"A baby?" said Mr. Chipman.

"Soon. Maybe this very week." Stephen laughed. "You can imagine the excitement at our house, the womenfolk clucking like a parcel of hens. I hope it's a boy—for Uncle Edward's sake; he wants a son. Auntie and Mother and Sarah are hoping for a girl, so they can dress it up in ruffles."

"You don't think," said Mr. Chipman slowly, gazing at his pen, "that the birth of a child to Mr. Fisk may possibly alter his attitude toward the career you seemed to have mapped out in such detail?"

"No, sir. Why? How could it?"

Mr. Chipman did not answer directly. He said, "In that case—"

and with the sentence unfinished, dipped into the inkpot and scratched briefly on the slip of paper. "A certificate admitting you to my autumn classes," he said, folding the paper.

"Thank you, sir!" Stephen put the precious slip into his pocket.

"You will note that the tuition fees are payable in advance."

"I'll have the money here tomorrow, Mr. Chipman."

"There's no rush. Any time that's convenient for you, and for Mr. Fisk."

"It'll be tomorrow, sir. I like to get things *fixed.*"

Mr. Chipman leaned back in his chair. "I must say, Stephen, that though I don't share your enthusiasm for politics—or for Andrew Jackson of Tennessee—I am convinced of your intelligence and sincerity. In fact, I've seldom met a lad who knows his aims in life more positively. I feel that, as a pupil, you'll be a credit to me."

"Well, I'll try!" Stephen exclaimed. "I'll surely try!"

The Fisk farm was three miles distant from Brandon, reached by a narrow road that sloped uphill and down, between groves of oak and elm trees, just leafing out, and fenced fields faintly tinged with green.

Stephen trotted briskly, for the sun was sinking and shadows lengthened. He was late—late and all the evening chores to do! He thought of the chores: the horses to feed, the cows to milk, water and wood to be fetched for the washing and the cooking. But mostly he thought of his interview with Mr. Chipman, and his heart was light at the memory of it.

Yes, the afternoon had been wonderful, it couldn't have gone better. Not that he had actually feared Mr. Chipman would reject him—but how pleasant it was to have even the smallest doubts dispelled. Now he could visualize the future as a journey in which each stage was clearly indicated, "fixed," as he liked things to be: the academy, then college and the law, finally the West with its limitless horizons and enticing opportunities.

"I'll tell Mother and Sarah," he muttered. "Uncle Edward and Auntie, everybody at home."

As he climbed the last hill, he saw the farmhouse, big and steep-roofed, a lamp gleaming in the kitchen window. He began to run, the load of books banging against his ribs. The kitchen door was ajar; he burst through it, shouting.

"Mother! Where are you? Sarah!"

They were right there. At the stove, Mother was stirring a kettle that smelled deliciously of beef stew. Sarah, a slim, pretty girl of eighteen, with pink cheeks and a coronet of smooth brown braids, was perched on a stool, spreading frosting on a cake fresh from the oven. They both looked up and smiled at him.

"It's nearly six o'clock, Stephen," Mother said. "Suppertime. You must have stopped in the village?"

"Yes, ma'am. Yes, I did—"

"We thought you'd never come," said Sarah. "And we have news for you. The most amazing news!"

"Oh?"

"Edward Fisk Junior," Sarah announced.

"What? The baby?"

She nodded. "Born at noon today, while you were at school."

"A lovely baby," Mother said. "Perfectly normal."

"Perfectly darling!" said Sarah.

"Well, this *is* news. It—it takes the wind out of my sails." Stephen hung his cap and jacket on pegs in the corner closet. "Is Auntie—?"

"She's fine," Mother said. "Edward is upstairs with her now."

"I'll bet he's strutting like a turkey cock."

"Uncle Edward's mighty proud," Sarah said, laughing, "and somehow *different*. You'll see!"

"But what were you doing in the village, Stephen?" Mother asked.

"Oh, nothing much." He felt that his own news was trifling by comparison. "I went to the academy and Mr. Chipman accepted me for the fall term—"

They interrupted him with cries of joy, and Sarah slid from her stool to hug her brother. "Nothing much?" she mocked. "Of course it is, you dear silly creature!"

Just then Edward Fisk came into the room, not strutting, but walking with a self-conscious dignity. He was a sparely built man, with a weathered countenance and shrewd gray eyes under heavy brows.

"Congratulations, Uncle Edward," Stephen said, hastening to shake his hand.

Mr. Fisk smiled. "The Lord has blessed me with a son," he said. "I am happy and grateful."

"We're all happy today, Edward," Mother declared. "Stephen, tell your uncle about the academy."

"Well, I saw Mr. Chipman and he signed me up as a pupil—"

Mr. Fisk uttered a strange little sound of disapproval. His smile had faded; he looked from his nephew to his sister. "I reckon this was your idea, Sally."

"No, no!" Stephen protested. "It was mine, Uncle Edward. Mother didn't know I was going."

"And I don't know that we can afford old Chipman's school. It's for rich folks, the fees outlandish high. We're not rich. We can't waste money on luxuries. Anyway, not now."

There was a painful little silence broken by Mother. "But we're not poor, Edward! Nor is education a luxury!"

"Never mind, Mother," Stephen said quickly, for she was flushed; she seemed confused, vaguely alarmed. "Never mind, we don't have to talk about it this very minute. Isn't supper ready? I'm hungry. Aren't you hungry, Uncle Edward? Let's eat our supper."

"Yes, let's," said Mr. Fisk. "You're a sensible boy, Steve, you always have been sensible. We'll eat and talk afterward, you and I. Out in the barn, eh? Where we won't disturb my wife and child."

# 2

## SOME DECISIONS

"Yesterday I had one boy to think of, now I've got two. That's the way of it, Steve," said Mr. Fisk. "I've laid by a nest egg of cash, but if your mother thinks I'm going to draw on it for your tuition at Chipman's, she's mistaken. I know a thriftier use for it."

They were in the barn, Stephen and his Uncle Edward, seated on upended nail kegs. A lantern on the harness box shed a pool of light, yellow as butter, on the plank floor. The air was redolent of hay and dust. The horses moving in their stalls made soft brushing noises.

Stephen thought that, for a quiet person, Uncle Edward was finding a great deal to say this evening. And, as Sarah had observed, he was somehow different.

"Nobody could accuse me of neglecting my sister Sally or her children." Uncle Edward plucked a stick of pine wood from the kindling basket and began to whittle. He was an expert whittler; his knife blade flashed and the stick took shape as a miniature canoe. "Ever since I've managed the farm, it's prospered. Hasn't it?"

"Yes, sir." Stephen picked up a stick of the pine and whittled too, though not so fast nor so well as Uncle Edward.

"I've looked out for you and Sarah as if you were my own young'uns. You've had a good home, good clothes and food. *And* schooling. The fact is, Steve, you've already had eight years of book learning."

"Yes, sir. But I've been planning—"

"Oh, those fancy plans of yours and Sally's!" Uncle Edward wagged his head. "College, a law practice in the West. Why the dickens do you hanker to go West?"

"I don't know," Stephen answered frankly. "I just know it's where I belong."

"You belong here in Vermont, laddie."

"You've never said so."

"I've not said yea or nay, never had cause until now to speak my piece." Uncle Edward whittled diligently; the little canoe grew, it would make a pretty toy for the baby. "Fred Simpkin is selling his forty acres t'other side of our apple orchard. Selling cheap. Fred's bone-lazy, he hasn't cultivated the land as he should. I mean to buy it, put in a stand of wheat and get a bumper crop. That's *my* plan, Stephen, to buy Simpkin's idle forty, then some-body else's, enlarge the Fisk farm bit by bit. For my son and for Sally's son. Someday you boys will be partners, as your mother and I have been. A family property, and fifty per cent of it yours. I've never cheated Sally, nor will I ever cheat you."

"I know you wouldn't cheat Mother or me—or anyone." Stephen paused. The trouble was that the prospect of being a farmer, even with fifty per cent of an enormous property, held no charms for him. "Couldn't you buy the Simpkin's field with some of the nest egg money and—and let me have what's left for my academy fees? It'd be a loan. I'd pay you back."

"I've never lent a penny in my life. I'm against loans, in principle. No," said Uncle Edward. "I don't like having to refuse you, Stephen. But you're sensible, you'll soon get reconciled to this, and see the wisdom of it."

Stephen was tired of being told that he was sensible. "I think

Mother will be disappointed."

"Probably she will. That won't worry me." Uncle Edward's knife clicked shut; the little canoe was completed. "Sally's a capable woman, most ways, but all women are fools about business. Naturally so, they have no truck with it, and shouldn't."

"Still, the farm is half hers—"

"And what would she have done with her half if I hadn't run it for her?" Uncle Edward asked reasonably, getting to his feet. "I've held the purse strings and I'll go on holding them. Well, everything's settled and I'm off to bed. Good night."

Stephen sighed and threw his pine stick into the basket. "Good night," he said.

The kitchen was empty when he returned to it. The supper dishes had been washed, the floor swept. He supposed that his mother and Sarah had gone to their room, and his impulse was to follow at once and give them an account of his hour with Uncle Edward in the barn. But it would distress them.

I'll wait till morning, he thought.

His own small room was in the attic, under the gabled eaves. He undressed and got into bed. Presently he heard Uncle Edward's firm tread on the stairs, the closing of a door, then the thin, quavering sound of the baby's cry and the murmur of Auntie's soothing voice. From his window he could see a patch of moonlit sky; occasionally the black branches of the old elm tree tapped on the pane. He found that he wasn't sleepy. Propped on his pillow, he meditated.

How stupid he had been to assume that Uncle Edward's ideas would coincide with his! Perhaps it was always stupid to rely on someone else. . . . I must rely on myself! Stephen thought. Because, whatever Uncle Edward might say, everything wasn't settled. Not by a long chalk! He'd never be reconciled to Uncle

Edward's decision. He was young and strong, he had health, brains and a streak of stubbornness.

He heard the parlor clock chime ten, the tap-tapping of the elm branches, and saw his door cautiously opening, the flicker of a candle, and Mother and Sarah, clad in flannel gowns and nightcaps, on the threshold.

"Stephen? Are you awake?"

"Yes. Come in. You look like two ghosts."

They sat on the edge of his bed. Sarah blew out the candle and whispered, "We've been so anxious. What did Uncle Edward say?"

He told them, adding: "I didn't beg for the money. I'd never beg for something I'm entitled to. And I'll go to the academy. I'll get a job and save my earnings. I can do it—and I will!"

"Oh, dear!" Sarah wailed. "Uncle Edward is a *wretch*."

"Hush, Sarah," Mother said. "A job? What kind, Stephen?"

"Carpenter work. I've done a lot of that," he answered. "I'm handy with tools."

"But is there a shop in Brandon?"

"No, but there's one in Middlebury. Nahum Parker is the proprietor."

"Nahum Parker?" Mother repeated. "He was a patient of your father's."

"He may need an apprentice. If not, I'll go on to the next town. Somebody will hire me."

"Oh, I don't want you to leave home!" said Sarah.

"Well, I don't want to leave you and Mother, but Middlebury's not far away, I can drop in on you often."

"And this house wouldn't seem exactly home to you now, would it? I know what you mean. Can't Mother and I go with you?"

"No, no, Sarah," Mother said. "We must stay here. I'm glad Stephen didn't quarrel with Edward tonight. Family quarrels are such ugly things. And, of course, much of what Edward said is true. He has been good to us, and I have no knowledge of farming. If the Fisk land had been divided when we inherited it, I couldn't have managed my part."

"It's the baby," Sarah said. "That darling baby has spoiled your life, Stephen!"

He remonstrated. "Oh, shucks, my life isn't spoiled. And let's not blame the baby. It's just that everything's happened at one time—Fred Simpkin's field up for sale, my talk with Mr. Chipman—*and* Edward Fisk Junior."

"Yes," Mother said. "The combination. I think Edward must always have had a poor opinion of our plans and would finally have spoken his piece. We can help you with the saving, Stephen. There's our pin money, you shall have it."

"I'll make my skirts and bodices out of flour sacks!" said Sarah. "And bonnets out of yarn, with straw trimmings. And I'll marry a wealthy, generous husband who'll shower me with gold—and the gold will be all yours!"

He laughed. "Thank you, Sarah. This is Thursday, isn't it? Tomorrow I'll go to Brandon and tell Mr. Chipman I'm postponing the academy—but not postponing it forever. Then Saturday I'll go to Middlebury." He yawned suddenly. "Now that things are fixed again, I'm sleepy."

Mother kissed him. "We must all rest. Come, Sarah."

He started for Middlebury early on Saturday morning. Mother and Sarah went to the gate with him, and the farewell moment was sorrowful. Sarah wept and embraced him in one of her strangling hugs. Mother admonished him to attend church every Sunday and say his prayers every night. But when he was out on the road, his spirits soared, he felt brave and ad-venturous. Strapped on his back was his bundle of toilet articles and a lunch of bread and cold roast pork, and he entertained himself by reciting aloud passages from his most cherished book, *History's Great Dissertations.*

" 'Friends, Romans, countrymen!' " he declaimed to a flock of sheep browsing in a meadow and, as the frightened animals bleated and scampered away, he shouted in ringing tones: "Cowards! Cravens! It is the famous orator, Senator Douglas, who addresses you!"

He trudged all morning and at noon ate his lunch in a shady spot and drank cool water from a brook. Then he went on, reciting and gesticulating, and arrived in Middlebury at sunset.

The town was small, but bigger than Brandon. He gazed curiously at the stores and the houses, many of them old and picturesque, and at Middlebury College from which his father had been graduated.

The carpenter's shop was in a side street. A man wearing a leather apron and smoking a pipe was standing on the cinder pavement beneath a sign painted with the name: Nahum Parker.

"Mr. Parker?" Stephen said politely.

"That's me."

"I'm seeking employment, sir. Do you need an apprentice?"

"I might." Mr. Parker had a tanned and wrinkled face, framed in a grizzled beard. His eyes, bright as jet beads, sur-veyed Stephen through a cloud of tobacco smoke. "You're not a Middlebury lad."

"No, sir. I was never here before."

"Kind o' little, ain't ye? Not more than knee-high to a duck. Got your reference?"

"Reference?"

"Recommendation. From your boss where you been working."

"I've been at school," Stephen said. "This will be my first job. But you'll think I'm the best apprentice you ever hired."

"Bragging!" Mr. Parker exhaled smoke. "Nervy! You're a banty rooster—likely don't know one tool from t'other."

"You could give me a trial."

"So I could." Mr. Parker knocked the ashes from his pipe. "Step in."

The floor of the shop was littered with shavings; piles of lumber had a sweetish, aromatic fragrance. On trestle tables were rows of tools of a dozen varieties and weights. As Mr. Parker looked on, alert to catch him in error, Stephen hefted the drills and chisels, the augers, saws and hammers, identifying each one.

Mr. Parker squinted his beady eyes. "Ever made a cabinet or chest of drawers?"

"Yes, sir. Many times."

"Well, I reckon I could do worse. I'll hire you," Mr. Parker said, "on probation—no contract. You'll get room and board. My house is right behind the shop."

"Room and board—and wages," Stephen amended.

"Oh, no! It ain't customary to pay a green hand wages. I'll be teaching you the trade, won't I?"

"I've got to have wages, sir."

Mr. Parker tugged at his beard and stared. "A dollar a week?"

"Two dollars."

"You'll have to spell my wife with the chores mornings and evenings. She's a mite finicky, real cranky about how the chores are done."

"It's a bargain, sir! I'm good at chores."

"And not bad at bargaining, either." Mr. Parker chuckled wryly. "What'd you say your name is?"

"I haven't said. It's Douglas. Stephen Douglas."

"Hmm!" Mr. Parker mused. "You wouldn't be kin to a Doc Douglas I knew years ago over in Brandon?"

"Dr. Douglas was my father."

"And you never told me? Why not? We were cronies, Doc and I. He cured my lumbago."

"I didn't want you to hire me because of my father," Stephen answered. "I've got to make my own way in the world."

"Well, I'll be jiggered!" said Mr. Parker.

# 3

# THE APPRENTICE

Stephen's room in the Parkers' modest cottage was clean, but cramped and dreary. The furnishings consisted of a bunk bed and a shambling washstand with a cracked china pitcher and bowl. Above the washstand was a blurred mirror in which, as he combed his thick dark hair, he could glimpse a reflection so dim and distorted that he scarcely recognized himself.

He ate his meals with the carpenter and his wife, and he soon felt that Mr. Parker liked him and was pleased with his work. But he knew that Mrs. Parker was not—and never would be—fond of him. Mrs. Parker seemed to regard him as her personal servant, burdening him with menial tasks and errands that infringed on time he should have spent in the shop.

Heedful of what his mother had said, he went regularly to church, where he became acquainted with boys and girls of his own age, and joined the choir which met every Wednesday night. The young people of the congregation were friendly to him, especially the girls—they said his baritone voice was so melodious and his manners so courteous! Some of the boys were inclined at first to taunt him about his size; as a consequence he was frequently obliged to demonstrate his proficiency in wrestling and boxing.

One Wednesday night he came back to the cottage with his jacket torn, his cheeks bruised and his nose swollen.

"By jingo, if you ain't a sight!" cried Mr. Parker. "What you been up to?"

"Nothing," Stephen said. "It was Lorenzo Taylor. He called me a *tadpole* and tossed my cap in the ditch."

"And then what?"

"I dared him to shove a chip of wood off my shoulder. 'Go on, you yellowbelly,' I said. 'Shove it off.' And he did and—well, we had a little ruckus."

"Looks like it," said Mr. Parker. "I believe you'd ruther fight than eat, Steve."

"No, I wouldn't," he said. "But these Middlebury chaps have got to know they can't pester me. Lorenzo knows it. You should see *his* lumps!"

The weeks of spring passed and it was summer. Supervised by Mr. Parker, Stephen fashioned chairs and tables, shelves and cabinets. He was conscientious, and gratified when Mr. Parker observed that he had the "knack" for carpentry. He never complained and he hoarded his earnings in an old stocking—two silver dollars every Saturday!

But he missed his mother and Sarah, missed the affection that had always surrounded him. Though he had promised to drop in at the farm, he had no chances to do so. Sometimes he felt dull, dejected—homesick.

He was in this dubious mood when, one September day, he received a letter from Sarah.

"Deacon Caleb Knowlton is opening a carpenter shop in Brandon," Sarah wrote. "It will be a big shop, very modern. The deacon will have four apprentices, all of them to lodge in his house. Mother and I wish you could get a job there. We are longing to see you."

Stephen read the letter twice, thoughtfully. The weather was gloomy. For the last few days, work in the shop had been slack, a circumstance that Mrs. Parker had quickly turned to her advantage by demanding extra assistance with the chores. This same morning Stephen had been out, wading through slashing rain, fetching and carrying for her, and later had heard her say to Mr. Parker that "little Douglas" was a "bungler" and "slow as a snail." Mr. Parker had defended Stephen, whereupon the lady had punished them both by giving them a scanty and unappetizing dinner.

Stephen suspected that Mr. Parker was afraid of her scolding tongue.

And I am, too! he thought.

After supper, another dreadful meal, he showed Mr. Parker the letter from Sarah.

"So you want to quit?" said Mr. Parker.

"Not until you can get someone else. I won't leave you in the lurch."

"But you'd like to go soon. It's an off season. Reckon I can make do alone for a while. Would it suit you to stay the week out?"

"It would suit me fine."

"I'll scribble you a recommendation for the deacon. You've been a good apprentice. Most as good as you bragged to be!" Mr. Parker laughed immoderately at his feeble joke, and said softly: "And here's a hint for you, Steve. Don't never marry a nagging female."

Back in Brandon and armed with Mr. Parker's "scribble," Stephen was quickly hired by Deacon Knowlton. On his first Sunday, he hastened to the Fisk farm for a happy reunion with his mother and sister. He had been apprehensive about seeing his Uncle Edward again, but Mr. Fisk did not allude to

Stephen's long absence or to that crucial conversation in the
barn, and they exchanged amiable greetings.

"Uncle Edward seems quite as usual," Stephen said to Sarah.
"I thought he might be angry at me."

"It's you who should be angry, not Uncle Edward," Sarah
said. "But you never harbor a grudge, do you? You have a sweet
and forgiving disposition."

"I suppose he bought the Simpkin forty?"

"Oh, yes. And raised bushels of wheat on it! That may be
why he's so cordial to you."

"Sarah, *you* mustn't harbor a grudge."

"I try not to," she answered. "I try to follow Mother's example. She has never once reproached him for behaving as
though you were a poor relation."

"Do you think Mother is discontented here?"

"Well, if she is, she hides it. And she adores the baby—we all
adore Edward Fisk Junior. He's a little angel, and in caring
for him we forget our grievances."

Now that he knew how his family were faring, and that he
could see them every Sunday, Stephen went to work energeti-
cally in the new shop. The other three apprentices were older
than he; they were old enough to vote in the autumn elections
and were much interested in politics. In this year of 1828,
President John Quincy Adams was a candidate for a second
term in the White House. Adams was a National Republican.
The candidate of the Democratic party was Andrew Jackson
of Tennessee. Though most Vermonters were National Republicans, Stephen was delighted to discover that his three
mates at Knowlton's were stanch Democrats like himself.

In 1828, Andrew Jackson was sixty-one, a man of integrity
and great courage, known throughout the country as Old
Hickory. A lawyer by profession, he had also been a judge, a

congressman, a senator and a soldier—and always a colorful, controversial figure in the American political scene, for he possessed a fiery temper and an indomitable will that brought him nearly as many enemies as friends.

This was Jackson's second race for the Presidency. In 1824, with four candidates contending, he had polled the largest number of popular votes, but not a majority. The election had then been thrown into the House of Representatives, where John Quincy Adams was successful. Now Jackson was campaigning again, opposed by the New England states, but strongly supported by the South and West.

It was said of Andrew Jackson that no one could be lukewarm about him; he was both the most revered and detested of American citizens. Those people who admired him vowed that he had no faults; those who hated him were bitter in their hatred. The four young Democrats at Knowlton's had sworn undying allegiance to him—though quietly, for the deacon was a National Republican and would tolerate no praise of Old Hickory. They shared a bedroom in their employer's rambling house. At night, and in seclusion, they conducted sober political conferences.

Eastern newspapers were attacking Jackson by recalling to public notice a much-disputed episode in his stormy life. During the War of 1812, as a major general in the United States Army, he had brilliantly defeated the British at New Orleans in January, 1815. This was the last battle of the war. Jackson had not known, as he deployed his sharp-shooting militiamen, that only a few days previously a peace treaty had been negotiated by American and English envoys meeting at Ghent in Belgium. Word of the treaty would not reach the United States for several weeks. Jackson's one thought had been to crush the invaders and drive them from the country; to that

end he had imposed martial law upon the city of New Orleans
and had temporarily exercised the powers of a dictator. When
the federal court of the district ruled that he was violating the
Constitution, he had summarily ordered the arrest and im-
prisonment of the judge—but after the battle, the spectacular
victory and the proclamation of peace, he had been arrested and
fined a thousand dollars for contempt of court.

The question of whether or not General Jackson had exceeded his authority at New Orleans raged for years and never
entirely subsided. Now, in 1828, his enemies revived it with
the hope of preventing his election to the Presidency.

"We had a debate about it once at my school," Stephen told
his three comrades. "I love to debate! I was captain of the team
that was for Old Hickory. We said he wasn't guilty of contempt of court, or guilty of *anything*. We said that Congress
ought to refund the thousand dollars and enact a bill to erase
the blemish from his noble record."

The apprentices were somewhat awed by this grand language. "Did your team win?" they asked.

"No, we lost. But we put up a dandy argument! The papers
are playing a mean trick on Jackson. If I were twenty-one, I'd
not only vote for him, I'd be out on the stump making red-hot
Democratic speeches, making the fur fly. And if ever I go to
Congress, I'll see that the blemish *is* erased."

The apprentices felt that Stephen might well go to Congress
someday; it wouldn't be so strange. He had read the Constitution and could quote it line by line. He was little, but spunky.

Shortly before the election, the people of Brandon awoke
one morning to find their village posted with placards advertising the "Bloody Deeds of General Jackson at New Orleans." The
placards were tacked on fences, tree trunks, the walls of build-

ings. A customer scurrying into Deacon Knowlton's shop said they were samples of the Coffin Handbills which the National Republicans were scattering everywhere.

"Who put 'em up?" queried Deacon Knowlton.

The customer shrugged. "Nobody knows. It's like magic. But they'll sure scare the few Democrats in Brandon. Jackson's a murdering villain. He'll not get a vote in this county."

"Well, he won't get mine," said the deacon.

At noon, Stephen went out to see the placards. They were horrible, shocking. Bordered in black, with a picture at the top of six black coffins, was a story portraying Jackson as a monster of inhumanity who had brutally executed six soldiers charged with deserting from his New Orleans regiments. Interspersed in the story, to illustrate it, were more coffins and a caricature of the General cruelly thrusting his sword through the pitifully cringing figure of a militiaman.

Oh, what lies! Stephen thought. All lies! The placards must be destroyed!

As he went back to his work, he thought of his shop-mates. Should he involve them? No, there might be trouble. He would do it himself.

That night he got into bed clad in his underclothes, pants and shirt. His cap and boots were on a nearby chair. He pretended to sleep, to snore. Then, when the house was still, he crawled out of his blankets, retrieved the rest of his garments, slid over the window sill and down the water spout to the ground.

He tiptoed to the gate and paused to put on his boots. A dog in the neighbor's yard rushed at him, yelping shrilly. Ah, but he had remembered that dog! At supper he had slipped two cakes of sausage from his plate into his pants pocket.

He tossed the sausage to the dog—"For you, Rover"—and darted out to the street—and away.

The village was dark and silent. He searched it thoroughly, ripping the placards from their tacks, wadding them into packages, burning them in a little bonfire. As he stamped out the embers of his fire, he saw a man striding toward him—the Brandon constable, waving his club!

"Hi! Hi, you! What's this?"

Stephen swerved and fled, pursued by the constable.

"Hi, stop!—"

"I can't stop and I mustn't be tracked to the deacon's house," Stephen said between gritted teeth. "I'll wear you out, you rascal."

Through the streets he pelted, dodging around corners, full speed, his heart wildly pumping—then, when the constable had fallen far behind, circling back to Knowlton's yard, shinning up the water spout and sinking, gasping for breath, into bed.

Next morning the deacon's customer was in the shop to say that the Coffin Handbills were gone, all gone.

"Who pulled them down?" the deacon asked.

The customer didn't know. "It's a mystery. They just vanished. Maybe your boys had a finger in the pie."

"My boys?"

"The constable seems to think so."

"The constable's crazy," the deacon said irritably. "My doors were locked by nine o'clock and my boys in bed, snoring."

Stephen rubbed his aching leg muscles and smiled.

In December Andrew Jackson was elected President of the United States. Brandon's few Democrats had loyally voted for him, and the four apprentices at Knowlton's were jubilant.

"But I wonder about those placards," the deacon said. "They didn't just *vanish*. Somebody made off with them. Well, likely we'll never know who it was."

"Likely not," said Stephen.

# 4
## SCHOOL DAYS

When it was autumn again, Deacon Knowlton said, "You've got this lawyer bee in your bonnet, Steve. You better get it out. Every lawyer that's licensed to practice goes through a starvation period, waiting for clients. Seven years, so I've heard. D'you want to starve for seven years? I advise you to finish your apprentice stint with me—and in two years you can set up as a master carpenter."

Stephen listened, but was unconvinced. He had no more desire to be a master carpenter than to be a farmer, and one day in October he marched purposefully from the shop to Brandon Academy, and rapped on the white-porticoed door.

As before, the starchy maid led him into Mr. Chipman's library. "I guess you weren't expecting me," he said.

"Ah, but I was," said Mr. Chipman. "I thought you'd come."

"I'd like to enroll for the semester, sir." Under his jacket was the old stocking that contained his wages. He produced it and poured the collection of silver and copper coins onto Mr. Chipman's desk. "My bank," he said, "and my tuition."

"Well, well! And all earned by the sweat of your brow?"

"Oh, the sweat was nothing. It was the saving I minded. I'm not really economical. Just the reverse—I'd never skimp and scrape unless I had to. Now if you have a place for me—"

"If I hadn't a place, I'd make one," said Mr. Chipman.

It proved to be a hard place! He found it hard to resume the habit of studying, to tussle with the intricacies of algebra, geometry, Latin grammar. He was dissatisfied with his first month's grades, but he concentrated on his textbooks and the grades improved. The fact that he had paid his fees himself was known in the school; it gave him a certain distinction. He was athletic, adaptable, cheerful—"a good mixer," said the other boys.

He still went to the farm on Sundays, and often saw there Julius Granger, a young man from Ontario County, New York. Sarah said that young Mr. Granger came to Brandon on business.

"Business!" Stephen said to his mother. "He's a beau! He's courting Sarah. Oh, I know she's always had a beau on the string, but she's serious about this Granger."

In February Sarah told Stephen that she and Julius were to be married on St. Valentine's Day. "Julius' mother is dead, but his father will be here for the wedding. You must stand up with us, Stephen, as our groomsman."

"Thanks for the honor." He allowed Sarah to hug him. "Is Julius the rich, generous husband you were hunting for? Will he shower you with gold—and all the gold for me?"

"Oh, you creature!" she cried. "How can you tease me so? Well, Julius *is* generous—and not exactly a pauper. But if he hadn't a cent in the world, I'd love him just as dearly!"

Sarah's wedding was a festive event, but Stephen worried about his mother. "Won't you be lonely, Mother?" he asked when the bride and groom left for New York.

She shook her head. "Don't fret about me. I forbid it. Sarah will write to me, and you and I will have our Sunday afternoons."

Stephen spent the summer vacation working again in the Knowlton shop; his wages would pay for the next semester at the academy. In October he was back at his studies—and in November an astounding thing happened. Julius' father, Mr. Gehazi Granger, made a second visit to the Fisk farm and asked Mother to be his wife! And, what was even more astounding, she consented!

Mr. Granger himself imparted this news to Stephen. He came to the academy one day and took Stephen off for a stroll in the village. Stephen rather liked the look of Mr. Granger; he was a big man, frank and genial.

"I suppose you've never imagined that your mother might remarry," he said.

"Never," Stephen replied. "She's so old."

"Old?" Mr. Granger smiled. "Well, I dare say she does seem old to you, though she doesn't to me. And you think of me as a stranger; it's true, you haven't known me very long. I'm a merchant, Stephen. My home in Ontario County has been lived in by several generations of my family. I can assure you that as my wife, your mother will have every comfort—in addition to my care and devotion. She will enjoy a freedom that, I feel, she lacks at present."

"Well, I've thought of that, all right!" Stephen said. "It's worried me. Mother's very unselfish and Uncle Edward is—not."

"Yes. I've seen that she constantly defers to Mr. Fisk, even in matters which she should control. Her situation as a sort of pensioner in his house must greatly strain her patience at times. In my house she'll have ample means and can do precisely as she pleases."

For a moment Stephen visualized Mother, comforted, cared

for, with ample means to do precisely as she pleased in everything.

Mr. Granger was continuing. "There's an excellent boarding school in our county town, Canandaigua, where you can prepare for college—"

Stephen interrupted. "Oh, I won't be going with you and Mother. I couldn't afford it. I'm paid up for the semester here."

"But *I* could afford it."

"No, sir. Mr. Chipman once said I'd be a credit to him, so I've got to stay. Besides, I want to. We're organizing a debating society and I'm the chairman."

Mr. Granger nodded. "Well, come to us in the summer. We'll talk then about the Canandaigua school."

It seemed to Stephen that his last months in Brandon passed by at the gallop. After his mother's marriage, he was absorbed into the academy's daily routine, lessons and more lessons, intervals of recreation, the fun of organizing the debating society, then cramming for final examinations, burning the midnight oil—and the last day of all, Graduation Day. Mr. Chipman's handclasp was firm as he handed him his diploma. "I didn't err in my judgment of you, Stephen!"

He went to the Grangers' in May. Letters from his mother and sister had described it glowingly, but without exaggeration. The fine old homestead was flanked by green lawns and gardens; Julius' smaller house was only a quarter of a mile away. Already Mother and Sarah had made many friends in the neighborhood.

Stephen got summer work in Canandaigua, but there was time, too, for picnics and hay rides and boating on the beautiful lake. That fall, somewhat reluctantly, he entered the local academy.

"I wouldn't, if Mr. Granger weren't so set on it," he said to Sarah. "I don't like being indebted to him."

"Mr. Granger won't think of it as a debt," Sarah said. "He's a truly kind person."

Stephen agreed. "Yes, I know. And I'll see that he doesn't regret this kindness."

The Canandaigua school was one of the most progressive educational institutions in the country. The big main building had a square steeple topping a mansard roof; inside were the classrooms and, on the third floor, a spacious dormitory. Professor Henry Howe, the superintendent, was a noted scholar; the students came from all the New England states, a few from Canada.

From the beginning of Stephen's first semester, his boon companion was a boy named Marcius Willson. The two were inseparable, sitting at the same table in the dining hall, studying together, playing games of kickball and one-old-cat together on the athletic field. There was a debating society here also; Stephen and Marcius enthusiastically participated in its activities.

The amateur orators of Canandaigua wrangled tirelessly over the governmental policies of President Andrew Jackson, for Old Hickory was still a target of criticism, despised by the National Republicans. Stephen was the most dedicated—and noisiest— of the Jackson "men." In debate, he shouted and exhorted, his eyes flashing, his voice bombastic and theatrical. Some of the members scoffed in secret at "little Douglas' ranting"—but woe to those who derided him at the meetings, for they were sure to be engaged later in a fist fight or wrestling bout, in which Stephen showed amazing skill.

Another of his intimates was "Buck" Smith, whose father

was a druggist in the town. One day Buck smuggled a bottle of nitrous oxide into the dormitory.

"Laughing gas, fellows," he announced. "We'll experiment tonight. A purely scientific experiment—when Prof. Howe and his minions are all cozy in bed."

The experiment was made by candlelight.

"Who'll volunteer?" Buck asked. "Who'll take a whiff?"

Stephen volunteered. Everybody volunteered.

"We'll have to draw lots," Buck said. "I've got a sack of beans, all white but ten—and they're coal black and lucky. We'll fish."

Buck held the sack. Stephen fished and got a black bean. The sack went the rounds, then the bottle. The lucky ten inhaled deeply.

Instantly the dormitory was in an uproar. The lucky ten sang, shrieked, laughed madly, and were watched with profound interest by an appreciative crowd of "scientists."

Stephen scrambled onto a chair. "Gentlemen, I shall speak to you about our peerless President Andrew Jackson—"

"Oh, no!" groaned Marcius. "Not Jackson! Not now! Dry up, Steve!"

"Andrew Jackson was born in Tennessee—"

"You're drunk. Be quiet," Marcius pleaded. "You'll have Prof. Howe in on us."

"I'm *not* drunk! Andrew Jackson is a great Democrat—"

They silenced him by smothering him with pillows and shutting him into a closet until the fumes of the gas had dissipated. He came out unsteady on his feet but restored to sanity.

"Hey, Marcius, what did I do?"

"What I was afraid of," said Marcius disgusted. "You

thought you were a politician on the stump. You were awful, the worst of the bunch."

Professor Howe believed in fostering the ambitions of his students. Knowing that many of them hoped to be lawyers, he arranged for a series of mock trials in the dining hall on Saturday evenings. With the tables cleared and the chairs in rows, the large room had something of the atmosphere of a genuine court.

On such occasions, Stephen was always the star performer, either as prosecuting attorney or counsel for the plaintiff, achieving a renown that got him into an altercation with one of the school's lesser "lawyers," a burly youth whose intriguing nickname was Birdseye.

Stephen and Birdseye were never friends; after they had been on opposite sides of a "case" which was decided in Stephen's favor, they were foes. Birdseye said that Steve Douglas was an "insignificant, sawed-off little runt." Stephen said he would punch Birdseye's nose. On the playing field, screened from the sight of Professor Howe, they hurled insults back and forth, and would have fought had not Marcius Willson parted them.

Stephen was almost as angry at Marcius as at Birdseye. "Why did you stop us, Marcius? I don't thank you for interfering."

"But he's twice your size," said Marcius.

"He's a windbag."

"And a sneak, Steve. Look out that he doesn't sneak up on you unawares."

A few nights later, as Stephen was undressing for bed, he saw Birdseye at the dormitory door, peeping in around the edge of it.

Peeping at *me!* Stephen thought. Now why is that?

He glanced at his bed; the coverlet was rumpled. He felt under the mattress. Yes, the cords had been loosened and were dangling. If Stephen had leaped into bed as he usually did, he would have crashed to the floor with a thud.

He slowly took off his shoes and socks. Birdseye was still in the doorway, still slyly peeping.

"Hello, Birdseye," Stephen said. "Waiting for something? An earthquake? Sorry, but there won't be one tonight. Scat! Go peddle your childish antics somewhere else."

Birdseye sneered. "Earthquake? You could fall clean through to China and never cause an earth *tremble*. You're a pip-squeak, Douglas, a puny little pip-squeak."

"Oh, am I?" Getting up, Stephen dashed at Birdseye, grabbed and pommeled him, while Birdseye countered with blows to Stephen's jaw and stomach. Clinched in a fierce embrace, they staggered along the corridor to the stairhead—and then pitched downward to the lower landing.

Marcius rescued Stephen, hauled him into the bathroom and washed his wounds. He was a mass of welts, his legs skinned, his mouth bleeding profusely.

"Where's Birdseye?" he croaked. "What became of him?"

"He was knocked cold as a clam," Marcius said. "They're bringing him to with smelling salts. Didn't I tell you that Birdseye is a sneak?"

"And a windbag," Stephen said. "And a varment."

In December of 1832, as Professor Howe's students were going home for the Christmas holidays, Stephen had an item of news for Marcius.

"I won't be back here in January."

Marcius gasped. *"What?"*

"I've got a job as clerk in a Canandaigua law office."

"You're joking, Steve."

"No, I mean it. It's Mr. Hubbell's office; he'll pay me a salary, fifty dollars a month."

"But why—"

"I'm getting old, Marcius. I'll be twenty in April. High time I was independent, not sponging on my stepfather. I was independent in Middlebury and at Deacon Knowlton's. It's a nice feeling."

"But aren't you going to college?"

"No," Stephen said. "I used to think I couldn't be a lawyer without a college degree—and that's not so. Some lawyers train by reading the books and clerking. I'll stay with Mr. Hubbell until I've scratched together a little money, and then I'll hit the westward trail."

"You've always wanted to go West, haven't you, Steve? It's an obsession."

"Obsession?" He grinned. "Oh well, call it that if you like."

"But what'll your folks say?" Marcius asked. "Won't your mother fuss? Mine would!"

"Sarah will weep and wail, I guess," Stephen answered. "But not Mother. She'll understand. You see, she thinks I'm cut out to be somebody famous. Really famous. A senator, at least. Senator Douglas!" He paused, and added: "And, Marcius, the funny thing is that she's right about it. I *will* be famous."

# 5

# THE WESTWARD TRAIL

Stephen was writing a letter to Sarah. He sat on the deck of a steamboat that plied the muddy waters of the Mississippi River. He had left Mr. Hubbell's employ in June; now it was October, the weather delightful, sunny and mild. Trees on the distant shores were tinged with the colors of Indian summer, saffron yellow, orange and splashes of bright crimson.

His letter was long, for he had been composing it a little at a time, as he traveled. The first page gave his impressions of Buffalo and the grandeur of Niagara Falls; there were pages penned at Cleveland and Portsmouth, Ohio, paragraphs written at Cincinnati and at Louisville, Kentucky.

"At the moment I am headed for St. Louis, Missouri, the metropolis of the West," he wrote. "In my search for the best city in which to locate—the best for *me*—I have drifted farther and farther from my New England roots. But I shall see you and Mother again before any of us is much older. I shall stop off in Canandaigua on my way to Congress!"

He folded and sealed the letter. It made a thick packet; he would post it in St. Louis. He smiled, thinking how glad Sarah would be to get it. He felt relaxed and hopeful, content with himself and the world.

Of course, his purse was flattening at a rather alarming rate. Oh, well—

A man standing nearby spoke to him. This was Mr. Samuel Wolcott, a Missourian. He had chatted with Stephen earlier in the day.

"You said, didn't you, that you've been looking for a berth as clerk in some attorney's office?" Mr. Wolcott asked. "If you don't find it in St. Louis, you might see what's to be had in Illinois. My father lives in Jacksonville."

Stephen glanced up alertly. "Jacksonville? Named for the President?"

"Yes. A small community, population of a thousand, but enterprising and typically western."

"I like the name," Stephen said.

When the steamer docked at St. Louis, he disembarked, mailed his letter, then caught a boat that was bound for the Illinois shore. At Alton he bought a ticket on the stagecoach leaving for Jacksonville.

The coach was a primitive, lumbering vehicle; he rode on the box with the driver. He was jolted and jostled unmercifully, but was fascinated by the changing landscape.

This was his first journey through the prairie country. The miles and miles of rank green grass rioting over the fertile black soil were even more wonderful than he had pictured them. Patches of timber edged the winding creeks and rivers; the only dwellings to be glimpsed were rough log cabins, each one girdled by a protective grove of trees, festooned with bittersweet, honeysuckle and grapevines. Wolves prowled at night in the dense underbrush; bobcats padded stealthily. Squirrels and rabbits, birds of all sorts, skittered or flew before the coach's wheels. Flocks of pigeons shadowed the sky at dawn; wild geese skeined in a symmetrical V, honking weirdly, monotonously.

Stephen breathed in the tingling air. Oh, the West was superb!

"I'm from Vermont, an old state," he said to the driver. "Illinois seems so fresh—and young."

"Well, it is," said the driver laconically. "Younger than you are, I'll bet."

When the coach creaked into Jacksonville, Stephen got down and looked around him. The village seemed drab, not enterprising as Mr. Wolcott had said it was. Roaming the streets, he noticed the shingles of eleven lawyers. One thousand inhabitants —and eleven lawyers?

Maybe I should have stayed in St. Louis, he thought.

He had a dollar and twenty-five cents in his purse; supper and a bed for the night reduced the sum to fifty cents. By noon of the following day, he had talked with ten of the lawyers, none of whom wanted a clerk. They said Stephen had come at a bad time, Jacksonville was in a temporary slump.

"We had a cholera epidemic here in the spring," they said. "Cholera is the scourge of the prairies; we're over it, but everybody's hard up, paying their doctor bills."

But the eleventh lawyer, Mr. Murray McConnell made a suggestion. "Go to Pekin, Douglas. There's not an attorney in Pekin, not one."

"I couldn't practice alone," Stephen said. "I'm not licensed yet and I have no books."

"Oh, a license isn't essential in these little Illinois towns," Mr. McConnell said. "You can try cases in justice-of-the-peace courts. Books? Take some of mine. Yes, do. I want you to!"

With a heavy parcel of borrowed books, Stephen tramped to Meredosia to get the boat for Pekin. The boat was late. While he waited in Meredosia, he sold his extra socks and shirts for a handful of cash—unfortunately he must eat! When the boat was a week overdue, he heard that the boiler had exploded, wrecking it.

Well, no boat and almost no money. What now? Tightening his belt, he turned again toward Jacksonville.

He thought afterward that hunger must have sharpened his wits, for as he pushed on he had an inspiration. If he couldn't be a law clerk, he'd be a schoolteacher! He began to make inquiries about this possibility. But the villages through which he passed were either too poor to maintain a school or already had one. He walked all day and slept in a grassy hollow by the roadside. The evening of the second day, in drenching rain, he sheltered at a farm near Exeter and bedded down in the haymow.

The farmer gave him a ride to Exeter in his market wagon, but said there wouldn't be anything for him to do in that town: "They've just hired a teacher. You might see how the land lies in Winchester. And I don't want your ten-cent piece! Keep it!"

The ten-cent piece, Stephen's last coin, went for a bun and a cup of coffee at the Exeter Inn. Then, his pockets empty, his shoulder aching under the weight of Mr. McConnell's books, he plodded on to Winchester.

They were having an auction, or "vandoo," in Winchester that morning. The town square overflowed with people; furniture and implements were stacked around an elevated platform; chickens squawked dementedly in slatted coops; cows, horses and pigs were tethered to hitching posts.

Stephen skirted the throng and went to the small hotel on the corner, colliding at the doorway with a disgruntled-looking man who was stalking out.

"I beg your pardon," Stephen said.

The man did not reply. He wore a shiny metal badge hooked to his suspenders and he was frowning darkly.

Stephen went into the taproom. A wood fire crackled in the

grate; a table was spread with dishes of meat and potatoes, bowls of brown gravy, fat slices of bread and butter. Food! Giddy at the sight of it, he sniffed painfully.

The proprietor was behind a counter, swiping it with a clean cloth. He scrutinized Stephen. "What'll it be, sir?"

"I'd like to have a meal—and pay you for it tomorrow."

"Oh, you're broke, eh?"

"I'm short of funds at the moment," Stephen said. "But I intend to teach school here."

"You can't," the propietor said. "We haven't got a school."

"Well, you should have. Every town should have a school. I'll start one."

"So you know how to read and write?"

"Certainly I do."

"And cipher? Add, subtract and get it down on paper?"

"Yes," Stephen said. "Why?"

"There's some that can't." The proprietor gestured toward the commotion in the square. "You saw the vandoo? Folks can't raise their taxes; Sheriff has to auction off their livestock and truck. But Sheriff's not a cipherer and today he's got nobody to do the figgerin' for him. That was Sheriff you just bumped into. He's plumb riled, fit to bust."

Stephen brightened. "If I ciphered for him—"

"He'd pay you big. You scoot out and tell him you're a read-and-writer, he'll snap you up in a jiffy. And hey, take a bite of dinner; eat it on the run."

For twelve hours Stephen "ciphered" for the sheriff, who rewarded him with two dollars. For two more days the vandoo continued; in all he earned five dollars. Whenever there was a lull in the sales, he strolled among the buyers, introducing himself to them.

And he made purchases of his own, meticulously recording in

the "figgers" he compiled: "To S. A. Douglas, 2 penknives, 68¢; 1 lot of newspapers, 14¢; 3 linen collars, 54¢."

He told the sheriff that he wanted to start a school in Winchester. "I suppose the problem will be getting pupils for it."

"Oh, you can scare 'em up," the sheriff said. "You've taught young'uns before?"

"No," Stephen answered candidly. "I've been an apprentice cabinetmaker and carpenter, and I aim to be an attorney. But I know I *could* teach."

"I'm sure you could, Mr. Douglas," the sheriff said. "Give it a whirl."

His method of "scaring up" pupils was to go from house to house, talking with parents of boys and girls of school age. Three months of education for three dollars was the bargain he offered, and the parents thought the bargain was fair. Even those who were illiterate themselves wanted their children to have a little learning. Three months was only a smattering, but better than nothing!

When he had forty pupils, he rented a tiny brick building which was equipped with a potbellied stove. He added pine benches, a desk, a blackboard, a ferule and a birch rod. The birch rod was merely a traditional symbol; every proper school had one.

"I'll never use it," Stephen said. "You can't whip the alphabet into a child."

He would look back with pleasure on that winter in Winchester. He had living quarters in an alcove at the rear of the general store. He was snug and warm, and ate regularly. He had Mr. McConnell's books to study—if he wanted to study. But he soon had many friends in the town and many diversions. He went to church suppers, husking bees, taffy pulls. At the dances he never lacked a partner, for he was an agile and graceful "stepper." He went to weekly lectures of the Lyceum Forum, and sometimes made speeches to the members, who thought that he was a "mighty smart young argifyer."

Yes, it was a fine winter. He wrote to his mother that he was now a "real westerner, with western feelings and principles." He liked Illinois; henceforth it would be his home. He wished that all the Grangers would move to this splendid state where "equality and equal rights prevail and no man acknowledges another as his superior." He said that he was happy in Winchester, doing well with his school, might remain there.

But in February a printed circular came to him in the mail. Mr. S. S. Brooks, a Democrat in Morgan County, was sounding out the political sentiment in this section of Illinois. If there were enough other Democrats to make it worth his while, Mr. Brooks would publish a partisan newspaper in Jacksonville. He was scouting for subscribers.

Stephen read the circular and wrote immediately to Mr. Brooks:

> My dear sir,
> No one could be more eager than I to see your effort bear fruit. I will secure subscribers for your paper.

And after that, somehow, he was haunted by the thought of Mr. S. S. Brooks over in Jacksonville, rallying the Democrats of Morgan County. He couldn't rid himself of the thought! He had opened his school on the first day of December. On the first day of March, having dutifully given his pupils and their parents full value for their investment of time and money, he closed the door of the little brick building and took to the road again.

# 6

# THE "LITTLE GIANT"

In Jacksonville on March 4, Stephen obtained a license to practice law in the Illinois courts. The license might not be an essential, Mr. McConnell had said it wasn't; but Stephen felt that if he practiced at all—as he certainly meant to—he ought to be qualified to do so anywhere in the state. With this technicality behind him, he got lodgings at the tavern, returned Mr. McConnell's books, and then went to call on Mr. S. S. Brooks.

Mr. Brooks's newspaper office was very small and cluttered, and pervaded by the biting smell of printer's ink. On a rickety pine table were boxes of dull metal scraps and strips and bullet-like morsels of type. In one corner was an intricate-looking black machine, the press. Mr. Brooks himself was a man of indeterminate age, rather bald, with a green celluloid shade over his eyes. He had a pencil behind one ear; his fingers were ink-stained, and he was putting type into a narrow metal tray, which was a printer's stick.

"So you're Mr. Douglas of Winchester," he said, eying Stephen reflectively.

"I've come to live here now, sir."

"Sit down, Mr. Douglas. Just push that stuff off the chair. I somehow had the notion, from the tone of your letter, that you were older."

"I'm twenty-one. That is, I will be in about seven weeks, in April."

Stephen sat down. There was a white stone pitcher of cold coffee on the table. Mr. Brooks poured coffee into two thick white mugs and gave one to his caller.

"Stale," he said, "but tasty."

The mug was not quite clean, but Stephen took it and gulped down the coffee. As Mr. Brooks had said, it was stale, black and very strong.

"More, Mr. Douglas?"

"No, sir. No, thank you. Mr. Brooks, how are our political prospects in Jacksonville and the county?"

Mr. Brooks put a chew of tobacco into his cheek and said, slowly chewing, that though he had got his Democratic paper going, the prospects for the party were not exactly rosy. In recent years the National Republicans had declined in power and numbers, they were almost as extinct as the dodo, but the new Whig party had formed and was growing—and the Whigs were a menace to the Democrats of Illinois.

"We have eleven lawyers in town—"

"Twelve," Stephen corrected gently. "I am a lawyer."

"Oh? Well, twelve. And all of them Whigs except Murray McConnell."

"And me, sir."

"Yes, yes. Of course. And you, Mr. Douglas."

"But isn't Morgan County normally Democratic?"

"It was. It has been. Andrew Jackson polled a majority vote last year when he was re-elected. The trouble is, some of those Democrats are backsliding, they're not for him now."

"Why not?" Stephen asked. "We've never had a better President."

"That's what you think, and I do too," said Mr. Brooks. "But everybody doesn't. Some of his policies have been pretty drastic; they've alienated a lot of people who once thought he could do no wrong."

"Well, he can't! I don't know of a thing he's done wrong." Stephen paused. "Maybe we can stir things up a bit, get the backsliders back into the fold."

Mr. Brooks smiled. "How? I write my editorials. Democratic gospel. They don't seem to reconvert anybody. Maybe you have something else in mind?"

"Yes, sir, I have. I've been thinking about it for months."

"Oh?"

"I think we ought to get Morgan County to give President Jackson a vote of confidence. Let me tell you—"

Mr. Brooks blinked. "Well, that *is* something. Something big! Just a minute. I'll send for McConnell. Murray will want to hear it."

When Mr. McConnell came in, Mr. Brooks motioned him to a chair. "You know Mr. Stephen Douglas, Murray? He's got a scheme."

"I haven't worked it all out yet—"

"Go on," said Mr. Brooks. "What's the gist of it?"

Stephen outlined his scheme. He said that in all small towns, and surely in Jacksonville also, Saturday was the busiest day of the week, the day when farmers brought in their fruit, vegetables and poultry to the market, and civilians were in the streets, buying, trading or merely loitering in the square. Why not hold a public meeting in the Morgan County Courthouse some Saturday—and soon!—where resolutions approving President Jackson's policies would be read aloud and the populace asked to endorse them?

"The Democrats will come," Stephen said. "And the Whigs will be nosing in, if only to see what devilment we have up our sleeves."

"A vote of confidence?" Mr. McConnell was skeptical. "We'd never get it. We would provoke a cyclone that would ruin the party."

Mr. Brooks drank another cup of cold coffee. "I don't know about that, Murray. This young man may have hit the nail on the head. I don't see the harm in stirring things up. The Whigs have public meetings in the courthouse. They're going to have one next week."

"Next week?" Stephen said. "Then we ought to have ours this Saturday."

"It's not feasible," Mr. McConnell said. "If you have it, I'll help—as much as I can. But I'm not for it."

"Well, I am." Mr. Brooks took off his green eyeshade. "Yes, sir! Nothing ventured, nothing gained. The Whigs are already out, raising Cain, blowing up steam for the fall elections, and they've got some good candidates running for the legislature. There's Old Abe over in Sangamon County. He ran last time and got licked. They say he's running again."

"That's Abraham Lincoln, Douglas," Mr. McConnell said: "Lincoln keeps the store in New Salem. He's not old, really; three or four years your senior."

"But he's plain," said Mr. Brooks. "Plain as an old shoe. No beauty—a tall, gaunt, hulking fellow. Honest, though, and witty; always has a story or anecdote to tell."

"Lincoln's quite a man," said Mr. McConnell. "Everybody likes him, even the Democrats. A self-made, self-educated man—"

"And ambitious!" Mr. Brooks ejaculated. "Ambitious as all

get-out. You'll probably cross paths with him one of these days, Douglas."

Stephen felt that the conversation was digressing. He was not concerned about a New Salem storekeeper whom he had never seen. He said, "Now, about our meeting, Mr. Brooks. We must advertise it. Can you print up some handbills?"

"Oh, yes. As many as you want. I have some nice cards, just the thing."

"Good! Then I'll distribute them through the town and county. Would you like me to write the resolutions?"

"Yes, go on and write the resolutions. Let's see what you can do."

"And read them?"

"No," said Mr. Brooks. "Our people don't know you, Douglas; they wouldn't listen to you. I'll get some prominent Jacksonville Democrat to do the reading."

On Saturday Stephen watched the crowd swarming into the courthouse. He wondered whether it was a Democratic crowd or one liberally peppered with scornful Whigs who had come because they were curious, or to ridicule Andrew Jackson. He wondered about the resolutions he had prepared, laboring over them. Would they be effective?

By noon every seat was taken. Stephen had a chair on the rostrum beside Mr. Brooks.

"A great turnout, isn't it?" Mr. Brooks said. "Magnificent! And hundreds who couldn't squeeze in."

The meeting was to convene at two o'clock, but at that hour the man who was to read the resolutions hadn't arrived. Mr. Brooks peered around anxiously. "Where the deuce is he?" he said. Fifteen minutes went by; the people were getting restive;

they squirmed, yawned, whistled. Mr. McConnell had been at the door; now he hurried to the rostrum, muttered something in Mr. Brooks's ear—and Mr. Brooks looked dismayed. The prominent Jacksonville Democrat had sent a message: Mr. Brooks must excuse him, he was suddenly ill with indigestion.

"Indigestion! It's sudden cowardice!" said Mr. Brooks. "But we've got these folks here. If we don't go on, the whole thing's a farce."

"I'll read the resolutions," Stephen said.

"You? Oh, no!"

"They're mine. I wrote them and I'll read them."

"You can't, Douglas," said Mr. McConnell. "You'll be hooted at."

But Stephen was up and at the lectern, pounding the gavel— and realizing that this was what he had wanted to do all along.

The crowd murmured and then was quiet, staring.

"I have in my hand," he said, "a document that all good Democrats, indeed all American patriots, will wish to endorse. It is an expression of confidence in our President, the man who guides our destiny as a nation."

Slowly and distinctly he read the resolutions, explained them one by one, and asked that they be voted on. As he waited for some response, he was acutely conscious of the murmuring that had begun again: "Who *is* the little tyke? Mr. Half Pint, eh? Mr. Small Change! . . . A furriner, ain't he? Look at those purty blue eyes, that mane o' black hair. And his voice—like a foghorn! No, like a preacher! . . ."

He waited, and Mr. Josiah Lamborn, one of Jacksonville's foremost Whigs, hastened to the rostrum. Pushing Stephen aside, Mr. Lamborn launched into a tirade, condemning the resolutions, the Democratic President, the Democratic party— and this brash meddler in Morgan County affairs, this "Yankee intruder." Mr. Lamborn was deft and sarcastic; but even as he stepped down, Stephen was back at the rostrum, wielding the gavel and replying.

It was an impassioned speech that he made, defending Andrew Jackson, the Democrats, himself included, and insisting on a ratification of the resolutions. And he knew, for he could see, that the people were listening to him respectfully—yes, spellbound! As he ended, with an eloquent tribute to Jackson, the applause burst forth, wave upon wave.

Then Mr. Brooks, looking somewhat stupefied, rose and called for a vote. The resolutions were passed—and Mr. Lamborn, incensed, left the room and the courthouse.

"Well," said Mr. Brooks. "Well, Douglas!"

But Stephen was not on the rostrum now. He had been lifted to the shoulders of shouting men from the audience, who bore him out of the building, into the square and all around it.

"Here he is, folks!" they shouted. "The High-combed Cock. *The Little Giant*."

# 7

# FIRST STEPS ON A LADDER

"There's never been anything like it in this neck o' the woods," said Mr. Brooks later. "From Mr. Half Pint to the Little Giant in one jump. Makes you feel dizzy, eh, Douglas?"

Yes, Stephen was rather dizzy, the jump had been so quick and unforeseen. Of course, he had infuriated the Whigs; their newspapers blasted and lambasted him. But it wasn't to be denied that now he was known in the town and the county, and in a few months he had hosts of friends, some clients, the beginnings of political influence and a law practice.

He eagerly cultivated these new friends. He mingled with them, learned their opinions, habits and way of life. He found that beneath a surface crudeness, they were keen and intelligent. Like himself, they took their politics seriously and were jealous of their rights. Whether Democrats or Whigs, they were all fiercely partisan. Political campaigns and elections were the salt in their otherwise prosaic and somewhat savorless existence.

And as Stephen furthered his contacts with the people of Morgan County, they were inspecting him, evaluating him— becoming fond of him. He was young, really not much more than a boy, but vigorous and daring. He was a Yankee by birth, but a westerner by *choice*.

And was he by nature a leader? Well, he seemed to have the ability for that!

In February, 1835, the Illinois legislature was predominantly Democratic. A public prosecutor for the state's First Judicial Circuit was to be elected. After some cogitation, the legislators elected Douglas.

Though he had wanted the position, he soon discovered that it was an arduous one. He had no time for his private practice, but as the state's lawyer, he must serve Illinois and travel over the district trying cases against law offenders in various counties. He was a novice at such work; he would have to make up for his scanty training by being industrious and thorough.

He rode out from Jacksonville and around the circuit on a horse hired from the livery stable. "I'd like to buy a horse, but I can't afford it," he told Mr. Brooks. In his notebooks he had jotted down a precept that he was never in future to forget: *Admit nothing, and require my adversary to prove everything material to the success of his cause.* Usually his "adversary" was a lawyer older than himself and much more experienced, but he was not intimidated. As Josiah Lamborn had said, Stephen Douglas was *brash.* And the older men learned, often to their discomfiture, that he studied each of his cases in detail and had an uncanny cleverness at ferreting out and seizing upon any flaw in the opposing counsel's reasoning.

The Whigs might laugh at him—they did!—and say that he was a "poppet," a "little tomtit," the "cat's-paw" with which voracious Democrats raked chestnuts out of the fire. Nevertheless, he was a good prosecutor and won more cases than he lost.

In 1836, John J. Hardin was nominated as a Whig candidate for the legislature. Hardin was an attorney in Jacksonville, very popular with the voters of his district. The Democrats cast about for someone to run against Hardin. Who would it be? Who would be willing and able to put up a stiff fight for the place?

Stephen Douglas, perhaps. But would he run?

"Yes," Douglas said, when the party's nominating committee came to him. "Yes, gentlemen, I'll run."

The campaign was tumultuous, and he loved every minute of it: the haranguing, handshaking and backslapping, the Saturday night rallies in village stores and rural schoolhouses, with hard cider on tap and brass bands blaring. Bustle and noise and torchlight processions, and in August the election, the "totting up" of ballots, the frenzied whooping of the Democrats: "Douglas has larruped Hardin! 'Ray for the Little Giant!"

Stephen wrote at once to his mother: "I must tell you that I am now a member of the Illinois General Assembly."

Vandalia, the state capital on the west bluff of the Kaskaskia River, was a town of comparative culture and refinement in this prairie environment, with five taverns, six boardinghouses, a grocery and dry goods "emporium," two print shops, a bookshop, a school, a jail and three doctors' offices. The statehouse was large and pretentious looking, but badly in need of repair, the inside walls bulging and plaster flaking from the ceilings. A new building was being erected.

Stephen's reputation had preceded him to Vandalia. As the young transplanted Yankee who had "larruped" John J. Hardin, he was an object of scrutiny and speculation. Whenever he spoke (and he wasn't averse to speaking—it was what he was here for!) his colleagues were attentive. In the sessions, his demeanor was grave, even solemn, but it was said that he could unbend and be very merry at times. The rumor was that at a dinner marking some minor Democratic victory, Douglas and his friend James Shields had linked arms, scrambled onto the table and danced and pirouetted the length of it, singing rollicking tunes and kicking over plates and glasses—to the delight of the other diners and the consternation of their host, who had to pay for the wreckage.

The most significant, if not the most urgent, measures acted upon by the Illinois Assembly in 1837 had to do with slavery, a matter that since the turn of the century had intermittently disturbed the harmony of the nation. In the South, slavery was deeply entrenched; southerners thought of it as necessary to their prosperity and wished not only to perpetuate the system, but to extend it into the western territories. In the North, slavery had no foothold, but northerners feared it and believed that the territories should not be opened to it.

Politicians of both sections had long regarded slavery as a political, rather than a moral, issue; the balance of congressional power had been maintained by admitting alternately slave and free states to the Union. As the nation expanded and new territories were organized beyond the Mississippi River, this balance was constantly threatened—until, in 1820, an agreement was reached: the Missouri Compromise, by which Maine came into the Union as a free state, Missouri as a slave state, and slavery was banned from all other territory north of the line 36° 30′.

Americans of that era had great hopes for the 1820 compromise; they said it would settle the slavery question forever. But in the ensuing years, southerners had complained bitterly that its restrictions were unfair, while in the North, and chiefly in New England, there had been an upsurge of feeling that involuntary servitude was in reality a positive evil, a sin against humanity, and societies had formed to combat, and if possible, abolish it everywhere.

These Abolitionists had the fervor of all true crusaders. Now they were publishing pamphlets and brochures demanding the immediate emancipation of all slaves within the precincts of the

United States. To retaliate, the governing bodies of several southern states had framed, and were sending out into the North and the West, resolutions denouncing such propaganda as dangerous and "diabolical."

Copies of the southern resolutions came to the Illinois General Assembly, with a request that they be endorsed, as a testimonial of sympathy for the South and indignation at the display of Abolitionist fanaticism. After only a cursory discussion, the legislators at Vandalia passed the resolutions by a vote of seventy-seven to six.

Stephen Douglas voted with the majority. He had never seen slavery in operation; his ideas about it were as yet quite unformed. But he believed implicitly in the federal Constitution, which guaranteed the rights of property. Slaves were property —at any rate, they always had been so classified, and there was nothing in the Constitution to say they weren't. Stephen thought that the southern states could not be legally deprived of a Constitutional right. He thought the Abolitionists were inflaming, rather than abating, the slavery controversy, which should be viewed rationally, not emotionally. He was inclined to think that the whole question of slavery was being overemphasized.

Of the six who voted No to the resolutions, one was Abraham Lincoln of Sangamon County. Lincoln was serving his second term in the Assembly. He and Douglas had met; as Mr. S. S. Brooks had surmised, their paths had crossed. Douglas knew that Old Abe, as a Whig, had opposed his election as state's attorney in 1835; at their introduction, Douglas had been polite but casual. And Lincoln, too, had been only casual, saying later to a friend of his: "So that's Douglas, is it? Why, he's the *least* man I ever saw!"

Some days after the vote on the southern resolutions, Lincoln and Dan Stone, another Whig legislator, spoke in protest of them. Lincoln and Stone felt that their negative votes had not adequately registered their dislike of slavery. They wished it to be written into the journal of the Assembly that they believed slavery was wrong, an institution "founded on both injustice and bad policy."

Several times during the spring of 1837, the legislators considered a bill for the removal of the Illinois capital from Vandalia to Springfield in Sangamon County. The nine Sangamon representatives, known as the Long Nine because of their unusual height, pushed the bill assiduously; the people of Vandalia fought it valiantly but in vain. Just before the session adjourned, the bill became law and Springfield was made the permanent site of the state government.

Douglas had sided with the Vandalia folk. Their new courthouse was nearly finished: what would they do with it?

"Public funds have been wasted," Douglas said. "I cannot condone this waste of the taxpayers' money."

But he himself was soon to move to Springfield. President Martin Van Buren, Jackson's successor and a Democrat, had appointed Douglas as Register of the Land Office, a job that Whigs said was a "juicy political plum falling into the lap of the wee Napoleon."

He resigned from the legislature and in July took up his new duties. In August he was invited to a banquet given by Springfield citizens to honor the Long Nine—and particularly Abraham Lincoln, who was the tallest of the Nine and had been the most aggressive in the skirmishing for the capital's change of location. Springfield papers reported that the banquet, at the Rural Hotel, was "sumptuous." Many toasts were drunk: to Illinois, to the Republic, to the Assembly's "sensible decisions."

Commissioner Douglas had been called upon for a toast. "To

last winter's legislation," he responded. "May it prove no less beneficial to the entire state than to *our town!*"

And Abraham Lincoln, lifting his glass, had exclaimed: "To all our friends. They are too numerous to be now named individually, though there is no one of them who is not too dear to be forgotten!"

# 8

# SPRINGFIELD SEASONS

When Stephen Douglas and Abraham Lincoln took up residence in Springfield, an odd—and for a time unacknowledged —rivalry began between them. They had been acquaintances before; now as neighbors they were often seen together. They differed in politics, but neither of them underestimated the talents and integrity of the other. Lincoln realized that Douglas was inordinately ambitious. Well, what of that? Lincoln also was a young man in a hurry to succeed. Douglas could not comprehend why any right-minded person should be a Whig. "But of all the Whigs around here, Lincoln is the most capable and honest," he said.

Springfield smiled as they watched these two strolling down-street side by side: Lincoln towering in stature, loose-jointed, wearing a coat rusty with age, the frayed cuffs exposing his bony wrists, his face thin and sallow, his eyes dark and brooding; Douglas short, robust and straight, neatly groomed in silk cravat, immaculate white linen and glossy broadcloth, his blue eyes sparkling with an unquenchable optimism.

Lincoln was very poor. All his earthly possessions could have been packed into a single drawer of the bureau in the drafty loft above Joshua Speed's general store. The loft was his home; he paid no rent for it. He boarded with the family of William Butler, clerk of the Sangamon Circuit Court: free meals, the Butlers

deemed it a privilege to have him at their table. He had formed
a law partnership with John T. Stuart; his office was shabbily
furnished and seldom swept or dusted. He had few clients; in
his leisure hours he was writing political articles that were printed,
unsigned, in Springfield's Whig newspaper, the *Sangamon
Journal.*

Douglas' salary as the state's land commissioner allowed him
to live in some semblance of style at the American House,
Springfield's best hotel. He liked good clothes, good food and
wine, expensive cigars—as he had long ago remarked to Mr.
Chipman, he would skimp and scrape only when economy was
necessary. His routine was not strenuous; he, too, had time to
spare. He had guessed that Lincoln was the anonymous Whig
contributor to the *Sangamon Journal;* in the columns of the
Democratic paper he replied to Old Abe with strongly flavored
Democratic articles, also unsigned.

Speed's store was a rendezvous for local politicians and their
hangers-on. Lincoln was always the center of the group that on
winter evenings collected about the log fire blazing on the hearth.
Lincoln was the entertainer, spinning his droll stories until the
room reverberated with laughter. Douglas, on the fringe of the
group, was usually silent, whittling at a stick of kindling wood,
now and then smiling at Lincoln's witticisms—the Little Giant
amused by the big one.

During the summer of 1838 the Whigs of the district nominated John T. Stuart as their candidate for Congress. Mr. Stuart
was well known to Stephen Douglas. In one of his earliest cases
as state's attorney, Douglas had tangled with the Springfield
lawyer and had trounced him badly; when, therefore, Douglas
was offered the Democratic nomination, he accepted it with
alacrity, saying to himself that it would be fun to take another

whack at Stuart—and, incidentally, to bait Lincoln who, as Stuart's partner, would be active in the campaign.

Douglas warned his party that he might not win the election. "It's a Whig district," he said, "and John Stuart knows every nook and cranny of it. But at any rate, I can make it hot for the scoundrels and keep Stuart on the anxious seat."

The candidates traveled on horseback through all thirty-four of the district's counties, even as far north as Cook County and Chicago, the ragged settlement which the Ojibway Indians had called the "wild onion place." When Douglas saw Chicago, the vast stretch of Lake Michigan, the churning, white-capped water, the wind-racked dunes and rocky beaches, he was struck with wonder—and with premonition. A harbor was in process of construction. Surely a great city would arise here, a great inland port for the West!

I'm going to buy some of this lake front, he thought. I'm going to have a stake in Chicago!

The traveling was tedious, but he felt that his chances of winning improved steadily. There were many people of Irish and German extraction in this area; they seemed to like Douglas' buoyancy, his dynamic speeches. He wrote to Sarah that these newcomers to America and thousands of young voters were Democrats: "Ask Mother what she would think if the people of Illinois should be so foolish as to send her prodigal son to Congress."

In a letter to his mother he said that the technique of his campaigning was simple: "I drink, lodge, pray with my constituents, laugh, hunt, dance and work with them. I eat their corndodgers and fried bacon, and sleep two in a bed with them."

The candidates spoke somewhere every night, often in joint debate. At such times, Stuart treated his youthful opponent civilly, though a trifle patronizingly, until one night when they were back in Springfield, speaking at an outdoor meeting in the square. The election was only a week off then; Stuart was very tired, his nerves on edge, and Douglas had made an assertion that angered him.

"That is a lie!" he cried. "Retract!"

"It is not a lie," Douglas said. "I will not retract."

Leaping up, Stuart twined an arm about Douglas' neck and dragged him down into the midst of the gasping throng. Douglas wriggled and kicked, but Stuart was a big man with a grip of iron. Dizzy and almost throttled, Douglas did the one thing he could do; he bit Stuart's thumb, sinking in his teeth to the bone. When Stuart howled with pain and rage and dropped him, Douglas remounted the platform and went on with his speech.

In those closing days of the campaign, the one thought of the Whigs was to beat Stephen Douglas at the polls. And on Election Day he was beaten—by the narrow margin of thirty-six votes in a total of more than thirty-six thousand. The Democrats instantly alleged that the ballot boxes had been robbed.

"It's a steal!" they shouted. "We want a recount!"

But Douglas would not ask for the recount. He felt that he had shown his mettle, had more than fulfilled his promise to make it hot for the Whigs and keep Stuart on the anxious seat, and there would be other years in which he could be his party's standard bearer.

He had resigned from his commissioner's post and said that now he would build up his law practice. "I am out of politics," he told his friends.

He was "out" until the next November, an evening when one of the friends burst in upon him as he was quietly reading in his room at the hotel.

"Steve, the Whigs are having a shindig over in the court-house. Cyrus Walker is orating like crazy—"

"Well, let him orate," Douglas said.

"But he's after us hammer and tongs, he's chopping us up to mincemeat! You've got to come and give him Hail Columbia! Hurry, Steve!"

He sighed and put down his book. "Oh, all right—"

Twenty minutes later, as Douglas was giving the surprised Mr. Walker a stiff dose of Democratic "Hail Columbia," Abraham Lincoln rushed into the courthouse, having been summoned by a breathless Whig who said that Douglas was on the rampage—"Poison, Abe! Pure poison! You've got to muzzle him!"

The discussion that followed—and continued for hours—was between Douglas and Lincoln exclusively, for Mr. Walker had withdrawn from it, as one whose popgun is silenced by the heavy artillery.

This was the first time the Little Giant and Old Abe had shared the rostrum, but it was not to be the last.

Springfield was a lively town. Most of its fifteen hundred citizens had immigrated to Illinois from Kentucky, bringing with them ideas of aristocracy and fashion. Ladies arrayed themselves in elegant costumes; fine carriages sloshed through the mud of the unpaved streets; lecturers and roving theatrical troupes attracted large audiences.

And what a splendid town it was for pretty girls in search of husbands! So many young unmarried men to flirt with and beguile! Joshua Speed was the prize in the matrimonial grab bag, for Speed was a native Kentuckian and quite rich. But the appraising glances of the girls and their mammas did not slight Stephen Douglas. He was handsome, educated; his manners were polished, his New England background was solid and highly respectable. Yes, Douglas was a most eligible bachelor; Springfield hostesses beamed as they added his name to their guest lists.

Douglas was one of six "managers" for the gala cotillion which celebrated the first convening of the Illinois legislature in the new capital. Since the American House was the scene of the cotillion that December night, he had only to don his swallow-tailed coat, his white collar and best black tie and sally to the ballroom, where the walls were gay with flags and bunting, and the orchestra, in a bower of greenery, was playing a waltz.

As he went into the ballroom he saw another of the "managers" just entering: Abraham Lincoln, looking ungainly and rather embarrassed in an ill-fitting dress suit. Douglas thought it was odd for Lincoln to be here; he was very shy with young ladies, and tonight the hall fluttered with flounced skirts, feather fans undulated, and above the strains of the fiddling floated treble voices and little trills of feminine laughter.

Ah, but now Mr. and Mrs. Ninian Edwards had arrived, with two more young ladies—Mr. Edwards' cousin, Miss Matilda Edwards, and Miss Mary Todd who was Mrs. Edwards' sister from Lexington. This, Douglas thought, should gratify all the "managers," for the presence of the Ninian Edwardses at any social function was a guarantee of its success. And, of course, it explained Abe Lincoln and his rented dress suit. Lincoln had come to the ball because of Miss Todd.

Douglas was on Mrs. Edwards' guest list; he had met Mary Todd when she had visited in Springfield the previous winter. He remembered a morsel of gossip: that Lincoln had seemed to be smitten with her.

It was said that Mary was husband-hunting. Two of the Todd sisters had married Springfield bachelors; why not a third? But the gossips doubted that she would want Abraham Lincoln. Oh, no, he was too roughhewn, uncouth! Mary's father was a Kentucky planter, affluent and proud. The stepmother who had reared her was quoted as having said that seven generations of gentle breeding were needed to make a real "lady."

Well, the Todd girls had their seven generations—and more besides!

Though Mary was not beautiful, she was vivacious, a dashing horsewoman, a good amateur actress. She could converse in French, play the pianoforte and sing lilting ballads in both French and English. And her clothes!—they were the marvel of every female beholder: gowns of creamy lace, Swiss muslin, embroidered satin, with stockings, slippers, scarves, gloves and reticules to match.

"Mary's father buys her clothes," the gossips said. "He goes to New Orleans to shop for them."

Douglas admired Miss Mary. She was animated, sweetly demure, but she was a Whig and let you know it at once. "I despise all Democrats," she had said. Still, she had been cordial to Stephen Douglas, and maybe more than cordial, a bit arch and provocative. Did she feel that the fact of his politics was offset by other factors?

Douglas had never cared to find out precisely what Miss Mary thought of him; he would never compete for her smiles. But now, as he saw Abraham Lincoln approaching her, he yielded to a mischievous impulse and hastened forward.

"Miss Todd?"

"Oh, it's Mr. Douglas," she said.

He bowed. "May I have this waltz?"

"Yes, I—I think so."

As they danced, he looked back at Lincoln, who was standing, bereft, in a corner. Miss Mary tapped him with her furled fan.

"And why are you grinning, Mr. Douglas? What is so comical?"

"Nothing," he said. "I'm just chalking up a little Democratic triumph, that's all."

Mary Todd did not go back to Kentucky this time. It was believed that she had quarreled with her stepmother and would now make her home in Springfield. She quickly became the town's reigning belle, and Mrs. Edwards hoped that she would marry Joshua Speed.

"Or Abe Lincoln," said Mr. Edwards.

"Not with my consent," said Mrs. Edwards. "But there's Stephen Douglas; he comes to the house and Mary sings for him. I think he'll propose to her."

Mrs. Edwards was disdainful of Lincoln's humble birth and poverty. Surely a girl of her sister's sophistication could not fall in love with him! But he was being very persistent, calling often on Miss Mary, gazing at her as if entranced, hypnotized by her airs and graces—while Mr. Douglas remained affable and aloof, seeming to wish nothing more from Mary than her friendship.

Exasperated, Mrs. Edwards said, "Mary, which of these young men cluttering up my parlor is to be my brother-in-law?"

Mary laughed. "The one most likely to be President of the United States."

"Abe Lincoln," said Ninian Edwards.

"Nonsense!" said Mrs. Edwards. "Stephen Douglas."

It was in this very month of spring that Douglas wrote to his mother, telling her that he was well, happy, immersed in politics and had no romantic attachments of any kind. And a month later, the Springfield gossips were stunned to learn that Miss Todd and Mr. Lincoln were betrothed.

In 1840, Martin Van Buren was running for re-election to the

Presidency. William Henry Harrison was the Whig candidate. Van Buren had not been a popular Chief Executive. He had carried on the governmental policies of Andrew Jackson and in so doing had inherited all of Jackson's enemies and made some of his own. Harrison was a veteran soldier, revered by his countrymen as the hero of the Battle of Tippecanoe, a noted general in the War of 1812 and, more recently, a statesman and diplomat. His running mate now was John Tyler of Virginia. "Tippecanoe and Tyler too!" was the slogan of the Whigs, roared stridently and incessantly, with vituperative jibes at Van Buren as "Van, Van, the used-up man!"

Douglas led the campaign for Van Buren in Illinois, touring the state, speaking indefatigably, imploring the voters to turn a deaf ear to the infernal din of the Whigs.

"Don't be misguided, don't be deceived!" he pleaded—though it was impossible to shout down the Whigs, and he had the presentiment that Van Buren was doomed.

But perhaps Illinois could be saved from the Harrison tidal wave. It was! In the election, only two northern states went for Van Buren; Illinois was one of them, electing also a Democratic governor.

The Whig newspapers said that Stephen Douglas was solely responsible for this reversal, this "calamity." They said, "Having maneuvered a Democrat into the governor's chair, Douglas is now a soldier of political fortune, awaiting his promotion."

The promotion was not long in coming. Douglas was made secretary of state and, in 1841, was promoted again to a judgeship of the Illinois Supreme Court.

"State's attorney, legislator, land office commissioner, secretary of state, Supreme Court judge. . . .

"And he's not yet twenty-eight!" his friends exclaimed. "The Little Giant! Watch 'im go, boys! *Watch 'im go!*"

# 9

# THE YOUNG JUDGE

As a judge of the Illinois Supreme Court, Douglas lived in Quincy, a town in Adams County on the Mississippi River. The courthouse there was new. The room in which he held his sessions was up a flight of steep stairs and rather small, but he felt at home in it. Included in the range of his jurisdiction was Hancock County, the domain of the Mormons, or Latter-day Saints.

The Mormons had come only recently into the state; their history had been chaotic. Joseph Smith, the Mormon Prophet, had founded his religious cult in Seneca County, New York, in 1830, and made many converts. But Smith's teachings and enigmatic "revelations" had aroused the suspicion of more orthodox folk who had driven him out of New York. Starting westward, Smith had stopped at Kirtland, Ohio, where again he was repulsed by the "Gentiles." In 1837, Smith had moved his "Saints" to Missouri and had purchased and consecrated a tract of land that would be, he said, the New Jerusalem. But most of the Mormons were Abolitionists; the slave state of Missouri would not tolerate them. After an interval of conflict that culminated in riots and bloodshed, the Prophet recrossed the Mississippi to Illinois, and on the river's east bank began the building of a city which he called Nauvoo.

The Mormons thrived in Nauvoo. They built homes, stores, a temple. They published literature, sent out missionaries, planned a university and organized a branch of the state militia. There were twenty thousand of them. Utterly subservient to the Prophet, they obeyed the laws he made—laws that might or might not be consistent with those of the state government. He controlled their votes, throwing his support to this political party or that, as his whim dictated, and at times determining the result of Illinois elections.

But here, as elsewhere, the Gentiles looked askance at Joseph Smith. He was capricious, grasping; his militia, the Nauvoo Legion, was sworn to protect only his church and his disciples; he boasted that he meant to become President of the United States. And the Saints were so clannish, so "queer," their customs and ceremonies shrouded in impenetrable secrecy. Soon the Gentiles in the vicinity of Nauvoo were saying that the Prophet was obnoxious, a nuisance and worse: "We must get rid of him. By legislation—or by any tactics available to us."

When Douglas was installed as judge of the circuit, the Gentiles were busily persecuting the Mormons, and a constable of Hancock County had arrested Joseph Smith, charging that he was a horse thief. Smith had been brought to Quincy and locked up in the Adams County jail, pending his trial. Douglas did not believe that Smith had stolen the Gentiles' horses, and he had misgivings about the temper of his accusers.

As he walked to the courthouse on the morning of the trial, he saw a crowd of people in front of the jail, listening to one of their number who stood on a soapbox and shouted at them.

". . . And I tell you Joseph Smith ain't no saint, he's a *fiend*, and it don't matter if he did or didn't commit this crime. The thing is, we've got to punish him for his godlessness, we've got to lift the curse of Mormonism from our bewtyful state. I say all his heathenish tribe must leave Illinois forever!"

A leering youth in tattered blue jeans sidled close to the soapbox. "You say punish the Prophet. What if the judge turns him loose? What then?"

"The judge won't turn him loose. Not this here litty-bitty new judge, no bigger than a possum. He won't dast."

"If he does dast, though?"

"Then we'll git the Prophet ourselves!"

Other voices were raised. "How? How'll we do it?"

"Why, by hangin', o' course. String him up on the gallows," decreed the soapbox oracle.

"*What* gallows? There ain't none—"

"Well, make one, you idjits! Fetch a rope."

Douglas went slowly up to his courtroom; it was empty except for the Adams County sheriff, who was pale with terror. Douglas glanced at the clock; ten minutes more and a guard would bring in Joseph Smith, the trial would commence. Glancing down from the window, he saw that the crowd had eddied into the courthouse yard. Several men were tearing planks from the fence, nailing the planks together. Under a tree lay a long rope, coiled like a snake. Five minutes, three—and he heard the thump of feet on the stairs; the mob stamped into the courtroom, overflowing it, packing the stairs, a sinister, scowling queue of irate men reaching out into the street.

Douglas sat down at his bench. "Sheriff," he said, "clear the court."

The sheriff coughed apologetically. "Your Honor, I—I—"

"Our proceedings cannot be halted by this demonstration. Clear the court!"

"Yes, sir." The sheriff coughed again. "Gentlemen! Gentlemen—"

The "gentlemen" erupted into loud laughter, yells and catcalls. They hustled the sheriff to the window and over the sill.

Douglas got up. The prisoner and his guard had come in.

Joseph Smith was shivering as the guard seated him in the dock, cringing as the mob growled viciously.

"You, there," Douglas said. "The redhead. Step forward."

The redhead, a strapping rowdy, glared. "You talkin' to *me?*"

"Yes, sir. You're from Kentucky, aren't you?"

"Well, what if I am? You want to make something of it?"

"I do," Douglas said. "Kentucky is a great state, the mother of great men. As you have seen, the sheriff could not clear this court. I'll bet ten dollars *you* could clear it."

"*Me?* Sure I could—"

"Then, sir, I hereby appoint you my sheriff. Select your deputies and get these hoodlums out of the courtroom. The law demands it, the country demands it, and I demand it."

The big Kentuckian was goggle-eyed, but he swung about to face the mob. "I don't *need* no depities," he bellowed. "Scoot now, you white-livered donkeys! Vamoose! By jacks, I'm the sheriff and I'm gonna clear this court!"

Sullenly they drew back a pace.

"You no-good scum, git out! The law demands it, the country demands it—and *I* demand it. *Out!*"

There were gestures of resistance. The Kentuckian doubled immense fists and knocked the soapbox oracle into the arms of the man behind him. The fists flailed, a second man went down, a third; a jawbone cracked, somebody moaned. The Kentuckian plowed toward the window; with the toe of his boot he hoisted men over the sill in the wake of the erstwhile sheriff. For fifteen minutes the room was a shambles—and then it was tranquil.

The Kentuckian dusted his palms and swaggered to the bench. "Well, Yer Honor, how's that?"

"Nicely done, my friend," Douglas said. "We will proceed with the case."

Joseph Smith's trial was brief. There was no one to testify on oath that he was or ever had been a horse thief. He was acquitted and told that he could go back to Nauvoo.

He wept and said, "I owe my life to you, Judge Douglas. They would have killed me."

"I want no thanks," Douglas replied. "You weren't guilty. In my court no man will ever be punished for his religious beliefs."

Douglas paid the Kentuckian the wagered ten dollars and took him to dinner at the Quincy Restaurant.

"It's been a grand day," the Kentuckian said. "You told me to clear out that murderin' gang and, by jacks, I done it. But how did you know where I came from, Judge?"

"I didn't know. I guessed."

"And how could you make me a sheriff, just like that?"

Douglas smiled. "Well, that was a little extraordinary—but so were the circumstances."

Some of the lawyers who practiced in his court thought that his deportment on the bench was too informal. They censured him for unbuttoning his collar in hot weather, slipping off his coat and sitting in his shirt sleeves, for sauntering through the courtroom during recesses, smoking one of his fragrant cigars and exchanging the time of day with acquaintances.

Some of the lawyers said he was too lenient in his rulings, others thought him too harsh. With certain types of offenders he was very severe. Illinois had a fugitive slave statute; Douglas enforced it rigorously. He had no pity for debtors or for men who evaded their financial obligations. He disliked the ruses and "red tape" by which attorneys often prevented the prompt trying of cases—for this he was dubbed "the steam engine in britches."

He frequently presided as a substitute judge in courts outside of his own district. Old Justin Butterfield, dean of the Cook County bar and the "big Whig" of Chicago politics, once said,

"Damn that squatty little Democrat! He's the best man we've had on an Illinois bench in twenty years."

In the summer of 1843 Douglas was nominated as the Democratic candidate for Congress. He was holding court at Knoxville when news of his nomination reached him. To his amazement, the attorneys, jurors, spectators and defendants rose in a body and escorted him out to the square, singing a campaign marching song:

> "The old black bull came down the meadow,
> Down the meadow came the old black bull. . . ."

He was elected in the fall. The Mormons had given him their solid vote, for Joseph Smith had proclaimed him a "Master Spirit," a brave man devoid of prejudice.

As he set out for the East, he was very conscious of the burdens he must assume. The people of Illinois trusted him; he told himself that he would never betray their trust.

He knew that the period was one of tremendous expansion in the nation's life—and of unrest which might presage great alterations. Immigrants were pouring in from Europe; long trains of covered wagons rolled from the eastern states into the West and Northwest. Railroads were weaving a network of iron and steel from the Atlantic seacoast to the Mississippi, American manufacturing flourished and foreign trade increased. Villages were becoming cities, traffic was brisk on rivers and canals. At sea, it was the era of the clipper ships, the most perfect sailing vessels the world had ever seen.

And social reforms accompanied the industrial foment. Laws were being enacted to modernize prisons and penitentiaries, to obtain more humane care for the indigent and insane, to regulate the sale of liquor—even to grant a few basic rights to women. But slavery was still the paramount political issue. The Abolitionists had swelled in numbers and intensified their outcry for the emancipation of all Negroes.

In Boston, the Abolitionist editor, William Lloyd Garrison, had spoken not only for himself but for every one of his followers when he said, "I am in earnest—I will not equivocate—I will not excuse—I will not retreat a single inch—*and I will be heard!*"

The struggle between the North and the South was aggravated now by the likelihood that Texas would soon be annexed to the Union. Texas was an independent state; under the leadership of the intrepid soldier-adventurer Sam Houston, it had broken away from the Mexican Republic, of which it had been a part. Now, with a constitution of its own, Texas asked to be admitted to the United States. Since its laws did not ban slavery, the far-flung area could be of incalculable value to the South, and southern congressmen were devising a treaty to speed the annexation.

This treaty would be opposed by the North. It would have importance in the Presidential election of 1844; and John Tyler, who had succeeded to the office of Chief Executive after the death of William Henry Harrison, would spend the last months of his administration in urging that it be ratified.

Douglas did not go directly from Illinois to Washington. He went first to Ontario County, New York, where his mother and Sarah greeted him rapturously.

"You promised to stop on your way to Congress—and here you are!" said Sarah.

"And what next, Stephen?" his mother said. "Will it be Senator Douglas?"

He laughed. "Perhaps. Who knows, Mother? I'm thirty years old and have learned not to count quite *all* my chickens before they hatch."

# 10

# WASHINGTON SCENE

When Douglas went to Washington in 1843, the city had approximately thirty-five thousand inhabitants but the appearance of an untidy, sprawling small town. Expensive and well-kept homes were jumbled among clusters of unpainted cottages, stables and sheds. Only two streets were paved, and those with cobblestones; sidewalks were made of gravel, ridged in the middle for drainage. A row of smoky oil lamps bordered Pennsylvania Avenue, the main thoroughfare of stores, market stalls and saloons. The Capitol was a bulky, wingless structure beneath a wooden dome; other government buildings were of an even more temporary sort.

And yet Washington had an atmosphere of vitality and briskness. When Congress met, the hotels were filled to capacity, colorful levees were given at the foreign legations, society folk entertained lavishly, and twice a week in summer the Marine Band played afternoon concerts on the White House lawn.

The roster of the Senate was starred with such illustrious names as John C. Calhoun of South Carolina, Lewis Cass of Michigan, Daniel Webster of Massachusetts. The House of Representatives also had a galaxy of celebrities, headed in prestige by John Quincy Adams. Defeated for re-election to the Presidency in 1828, Adams was now a congressman, the "Old

Man Eloquent" of the Whigs and the most venerable figure of them all.

Douglas felt that he entered the House at a very opportune time. A bill was just being considered that would remit the fine imposed so long ago upon Andrew Jackson for his contempt of court at New Orleans. Douglas' thoughts flashed back to Vermont, Brandon, Deacon Knowlton's apprentices, his own youthful vow to exonerate Jackson. Boldly rising, he spoke for the bill, a vehement speech that helped to pass it—and identified the new representative from Illinois as a person who would often have something to say.

But the next speech he delivered, as chairman of a committee investigating election frauds, incurred the scorn of John Quincy Adams. Writing in his diary, Adams referred to Douglas as an upstart, "a little man who raved out his hour" abusing the Whig party, "his face convulsed, his gesticulations frantic." In the heat of argument, Douglas had stripped off his necktie, unfastened his waistcoat. "His aspect," Adams wrote, "was that of a half-naked pugilist."

Douglas was never to read the Adams diary, but he knew that Adams and other House members had publicly called him a homunculus, a dwarf, a pigmy. He was always sensitive to epithets satirizing his size, or lack of it.

Well, he would make these new associates respect him for his character and ability, as he was respected in Illinois!

His seatmate in the House was David Reid, a young North Carolinian.

"Stephen, do you like to squire girls about?" Reid asked one day in spring.

He answered cautiously, "If the girls are pretty. Why?"

"My cousins, Martha and Lucinda Martin, are in Washington," Reid said. "I shall have to take them to dances, receptions, the theater. Stand by and lend aid, won't you?"

When Douglas saw David Reid's cousins, he was more than willing to stand by and lend aid. The Martin girls were very pretty and he immediately fell in love with slender, hazel-eyed Miss Martha. But did she care for him? And if not, how could she be *induced* to care?

He bought some new clothes, consulted his mirror, consulted Reid.

"David, am I getting fat?"

"No, not fat," Reid said. "A bit thick around the waist—"

Thick? Heavens, he must diet! So, dapper, dandified and dieting, he squired Miss Martha about for six wonderful weeks. He sent her flowers and bonbons, and was plunged into gloom when she and her sister went back to North Carolina.

"I'm afraid I'll never see her again, David," he said.

"Why not?" Reid said. "Come down to my place in June. It's not far from the Martins' plantation in Rockingham County."

In June, with Reid, Douglas visited the Martins. Martha's father, Colonel Robert Martin, owned hundreds of acres of cotton, rice and tobacco fields, and the slaves who labored in them; his pillared house was big and beautiful. Douglas was bemused by this glimpse of the aristocratic South, the southern patrician's pattern of luxurious existence.

"But it makes me despondent, too," he told Reid. "Martha seems to have a dozen suitors, all of whom have plenty to offer her. She'll never marry me."

"You haven't asked her to marry you?"

"No, not yet."

"Don't be fainthearted," said Reid. "You're probably the suitor she fancies most. Go on and pop the question."

A week later Douglas "popped the question." Martha didn't say she would marry him—but she didn't say she *wouldn't*. He would wait and hope!

In 1844, when Congress had adjourned, he campaigned for James K. Polk, the Democratic Presidential candidate. Polk was from Tennessee; Douglas went to Nashville to speak for him at a party rally. After the rally, Douglas with a group of Polk's friends drove out to the Hermitage, the home of Andrew Jackson.

Jackson was seventy-seven now, living in retirement, but still the idol of millions of Americans. Seated on a sofa in the hall of his picturesque mansion, he gravely shook hands with his guests as they filed past him.

"General," said one of the Nashville Democrats, "this is Mr. Stephen A. Douglas."

"Douglas?" Jackson's eyes brightened under their shaggy brow; he gripped Douglas' hand hard. "Sir, are you the man who addressed the House, vindicating what I did at New Orleans?"

"Yes, sir," Douglas said. "I made such a speech."

"Ah! Sit down beside me, Mr. Douglas. I desire to thank you for that speech."

Douglas sat down, and Jackson continued: "You are the first man ever to relieve my mind on a subject which has worried me for thirty years. My enemies have said I violated the Constitution of my country by declaring martial law on that occasion. My friends have said that it *was* a violation, but justified by the circumstances. Now, I myself have felt that had I done otherwise, I should have been remiss in my duty, a traitor in the sight of God and man. But I could never make out a *legal* justification for my course, nor has it ever been made out, sir, until you established that justification beyond the possibility of cavil or doubt. I thank you, sir, for your speech."

Douglas bowed and smiled. He would never forget how richly his hero had rewarded him.

Polk's election brought Douglas into the forefront of national politics. Like Tyler, Polk advocated the annexation of Texas. Congress had rejected the treaty sponsored by Tyler; but Polk, early in his administration, instigated a reconsideration of it, which Douglas stanchly supported.

Indeed, Douglas' views were even broader than the new President's. He believed that all the West and the Northwest should be incorporated into the Union; he visualized the United States as one mighty republic—"an ocean bound republic." But would Texas be a slave or a free state? This was the problem that lurked at the bottom of all congressional deliberations and was at length dragged into the open by southern proslavery "fire-eaters."

Douglas, in the House, was for a compromise. He was aware that the contention over slavery was not the unimportant thing he once had thought it, yet he still believed it to be a local problem that the states should manage individually—and never one that might impede the progress of the nation! "Let Congress legislate for the admittance of Texas as a slave state," he said, "and for the creating of not more than four more states carved from what remains of the huge territory. In any of such states lying below the old Missouri Compromise line, let the voters decide whether they want or do not want slavery; and in any states that might in future take shape north of the line, let slavery be prohibited."

Douglas' suggestion was hotly debated, for it pleased neither the fire-eaters nor the northern Abolitionist faction. But the resolutions enacted by the House in February, 1845, were almost exactly as he had phrased them. Within a few months, Texas would come into the Union as a slave state, and politicians of both North and South would remember that Stephen Douglas at this time had vouched for the legality of the Missouri Compromise's specifications.

And, meanwhile, Illinois was troubled again by the Mormons. Douglas went home to see what could be done.

In 1843, Joseph Smith had received another divine revelation. Angels whispering to the Prophet as he slept had told him that plural marriage was holy; though he had one wife, he must have several wives. Obedient to the angels, Smith had married a number of Mormon girls, and many of his disciples had followed his example. For a time the new doctrine had been kept a secret from the Gentiles of Hancock County. When, inevitably, the secret was disclosed, Smith's neighbors had recoiled in horror.

Plural marriage? *Polygamy?*

"Down with the Saints!" cried the Gentiles. "Persecute them!"

To shield and avenge his people, the Prophet had recruited and armed a company of men known as the Danites. Riding out from Nauvoo, the Danites raided and destroyed, and soon were tilting with similar companies of enraged Gentiles. As the situation deteriorated from bad to worse, Governor Ford of Illinois ordered Joseph Smith to go to the town of Carthage—where, said Ford, the dilemma could be arbitrated.

Smith had not wanted to go to Carthage. "I will not go," he said at first. But in June of 1844 he did go, and his brother Hyrum and other Mormon priests went with him. Since Ford had pledged that they should be safe in Carthage, the Mormons submitted to being imprisoned in the town jail.

On the afternoon of June 27, as the Prophet was reading and praying in his cell, two hundred Gentiles, their faces blackened with soot, battered down the door of the jail. Begging for mercy, Smith cringed against the wall. A rifle barked and he dropped to the floor—dead. Hyrum also was killed, his body riddled with bullets. Somehow, miraculously, the other priests escaped to Nauvoo.

The Twelve Apostles of the church had then named Brigham Young as their leader, and had dispatched the Danites to burn the barns of Gentiles, steal horses and cattle, ravish fields and orchards. For a year Hancock County was a place of constant and savage guerrilla warfare. The state authorities knew that the Gentiles were as much to blame as the Mormons, but the governor felt that now, once and for all, the Saints must leave Illinois.

"If they will not leave of their own volition," said Governor Ford, "we will eject them."

In the summer of 1845, a militia regiment of four hundred and fifty men was sent to Nauvoo to arrest the Twelve Apostles. John J. Hardin was the colonel of the regiment, and the governor commissioned Stephen Douglas as a major in it. Douglas, who had never before been a soldier (or imagined himself as one), came from Washington and joined the regiment en route. He was rather excited about this new venture.

The militiamen marched toward Nauvoo, and halted at the city's outskirts, where four thousand Mormon Danites, equipped with rifles, revolvers and sabers were drawn up in phalanx.

Colonel Hardin gazed at the Danites and frowned. He said to his officers: "The ratio here is almost ten to one, I think. If we attack, it will be a bloody slaughter." He paused and then said, "Major Douglas, select a hundred of our troopers, go into

Nauvoo, arrest the Twelve Apostles and bring them to me."

For a moment, Douglas looked startled. "Is that a peremptory command, sir?"

"It is."

"Then I will comply with it. You know, of course, that we will all be killed. I should much prefer to undertake the mission alone."

Now Hardin looked startled. "You prefer to be killed alone?"

"Yes. You seem to believe—and very sensibly—that it is better to lose one hundred men than four hundred and fifty. I believe it is also better to lose one man than a hundred."

Hardin was in a quandary. Stephen Douglas had been his political opponent, but they were friends. Hardin had thought of the Little Giant as rash, something of a daredevil, but always perfectly sane. And what was the alternative? To fling a regiment of law-abiding militiamen at the poised weapons of ten times as many desperate, lawless Danites?

At last, Hardin said, "Major Douglas, I command you to do— as you see fit."

Douglas saluted, clicked his heels, turned about and crossed the neutral ground to the Mormon lines. A Danite officer stepped out, a few words were said in low tones that Hardin could not hear. The Danite nodded; the Mormon lines swerved and opened an aisle between the ranks. Douglas walked through the aisle and the ranks closed again, blotting him from sight.

An hour went by—slowly for Hardin, who was penitent, thinking: I have done a terrible thing. I have sent Douglas to his death!

Then there was the sound of wheels, horses' hoofs. A coach came clattering out from the Nauvoo streets, a large and shiny coach, pulled by eight sleek horses. The coach stopped on the neutral ground, Douglas alighted from it, twelve bearded men alighted, and all walked toward Hardin.

"Colonel Hardin," Douglas said, "these are the twelve Mormon Apostles. This is Mr. Brigham Young. We have just had a very fruitful discussion. Mr. Young will read to you a covenant which we have signed."

Brigham was a stern-visaged patriarch. His voice was deep and sonorous as he read: "The Mormons have covenanted with Stephen A. Douglas to cease their raids and depredations as of this date, and to move bag and baggage from Illinois in the spring. . . ."

"I suppose you did it by mesmerism, Douglas," said Hardin, as the militia regiment marched away from Nauvoo. "Incantations, sorcery—"

"No, by arbitration and concessions," Douglas said, "by convincing the Apostles that for their own good, as much as ours, they would be wise to establish their New Jerusalem farther west. Brigham Young was the most difficult to convince. A handsome man, isn't he? A man of iron—I admire him. He wouldn't sign until I had assured him on my honor that the Saints will not be harried out of the state like wild beasts, but can make a gradual, peaceable exit. Those were my concessions. You see, Hardin, they are not wild beasts. They're people, and with many virtues. They can become good citizens, an asset to our country, artisans and builders in the West."

"But can they make such an exit?"

"Of course! I'll arrange it."

"You must have known that they wouldn't kill you."

Douglas smiled. "Well, I hoped they wouldn't. I hoped they would first listen to me. And they did. Some of the Saints are old side-kicks of mine. They remembered when I was on the bench at Quincy. I remember it, too."

Hardin hummed softly to himself. Among Illinois politicians, it was jokingly said that Stephen Douglas could charm the birds out of the trees.

Hardin thought that might be true.

# 11
# WIDENING HORIZONS

The voters of Douglas' district seemed quite satisfied with the "little man" who represented them in Washington, for in 1845 they re-elected him, and when Congress convened again he was made chairman of the Committee on Territories in the House.

During this session the boundaries of the Oregon country, which lay west of the Rocky Mountains and north of the forty-second parallel, were studied.

Earlier in the century, treaties between Russia, the United States and Great Britain had defined Oregon's northern boundary as the parallel 54° 40' and granted joint ownership to the United States and England. Since then the region had been sparsely settled by pioneering American farmers and British fur traders. The title of the United States to Oregon was vague; England's was even vaguer. But the American pioneers could say (as the Britishers could not) that they had gone there with the intention of staying permanently, not merely to exploit the commercial possibilities. In 1846, these Americans were claiming that Oregon belonged to them exclusively.

"We must have all Oregon or none!" they said. "Fifty-four forty or fight!"

Douglas warmly espoused the American claims. He thought the idea of joint ownership was impractical and could never be made to work smoothly. He believed in "squatter sovereignty"—

"popular sovereignty." Trail blazers, he said, were the rightful owners of any land they redeemed from the wilderness. He saw Oregon as a part of the American West; someday it would be a state of that peerless Union which would sweep from ocean to ocean. He fervidly echoed the cry of "All Oregon or none!"

But the Whigs and the more conservative Democrats in Congress feared a break with England, and Douglas and his cohorts were overruled. A new treaty was negotiated, fixing the northern limit for American possession at the forty-ninth parallel, thence west to the Strait of San Juan de Fuca and down the middle of the channel to the sea.

Douglas was crestfallen. Here was one of his chickens that hadn't hatched! "It is an error that we will rue," he said. "England has no right to a single acre of our northwest coast."

The Oregon tempest had scarcely subsided when the United States was embroiled in another boundary quarrel, this one in the recently organized state of Texas.

As a part of the Mexican Republic, Texas had been bounded on the south by the Nueces River. Now, in the spring of 1846, the Texans—and President Polk—were asserting that the state stretched farther south, to the Rio Grande. General Zachary Taylor was in Texas with four thousand American soldiers. Polk ordered General Taylor to cross the Nueces and advance to the Rio Grande, which henceforth must be held as the new state's southern and western boundary.

Not unnaturally, Mexico regarded Taylor's advance as an invasion and warned him that there would be reprisals. When he ignored the warning and crossed the Nueces, Mexican troops assaulted and captured a small detachment of his army.

Many United States citizens were not surprised by Mexico's hostility. "Nor is President Polk surprised," they said. "Polk wants a war. He is a warmonger!"

Whether or not such imputations were deserved, Polk wasted no time in announcing that Mexico had shed American blood on American soil, and in asking for, and obtaining from Congress, a declaration of war.

On May 22, bills were passed appropriating money for the war's expenses and for the recruiting of fifty thousand more soldiers, and soon the battles began. Mexico had the larger army, but the Americans had more and better guns and cannon, and they fought with a dogged valor that seemed to presage ultimate victory.

Douglas had voted for the war. He was for every measure to implement it. He would have enlisted with the Illinois volunteers had not President Polk said that the Little Giant could be of more use to his country in Congress than on the firing line. Douglas was for adding to the United States any portions of the continent that could be had!—and when David Wilmot, a congressman from Pennsylvania, offered a "proviso" that no territory acquired either by purchase or by war should ever be open to slavery, Douglas argued and voted against it.

Slavery was not now the issue, he said. "The nation is at war and the war must be won!"

In Illinois, where the war fever flared high, Douglas' militancy was as highly lauded. In 1847 he was re-elected to the House by a bigger majority than ever before. In that year, the Illinois legislature was due to elect a United States senator—and what was more logical than that the legislators, who were mostly Democrats, should choose Stephen Douglas? He had been a forceful and dominant leader in the House; these friends of his felt that he would do as well in the Senate. His ascent of the ladder had been swift.

"Yes," said his friends, "and he will go to the very top!"

Senator Douglas! He was thirty-four when he took the office, and in April he married Martha Denny Martin whom he had loved devotedly, and diligently courted, for four long years.

The sun shone on his wedding day. The parlors of the Martins' North Carolina mansion were decked with roses, jasmine and magnolia blossoms, and Martha was a radiant bride in her white satin gown and misty lace veil.

After the ceremony, Colonel Martin handed Douglas a legal-looking document. "For you, Stephen," he said.

Douglas scanned the document; it was the deed to a cotton plantation in Mississippi—the land, the buildings and gear, and also the slaves. He glanced up at Colonel Martin. "You know, sir, that Martha and I are going to live in Washington when Congress is in session, and in Chicago at other times."

"Yes, I know. But you should have a bit of southern property and the income from it."

"I can't accept so much from you—"

"But it's not so much!" Colonel Martin smiled. "Martha is my daughter, you are now my son, and I'm a rich man. I have several plantations, I can spare this one."

"No, sir. I—I can't accept it."

"I don't understand," said Colonel Martin; then, his eyes narrowing thoughtfully: "Perhaps you have scruples about being a slaveholder? Is that it?"

"Perhaps it is."

"But you're not one of those crazy Abolitionists!"

"No," Douglas said. "No, I'm not. The Abolitionists *are* crazy. They would disrupt the Union with their fantastic preachings." He paused. "I'm not sure that I can make you understand how I feel about slavery. Is the system good or bad, or a mixture of good and bad? The latter, I think, the mixture; and I would not vote it up or down. I see your Negroes here, well fed, in warm cabins. Would they be better off if you freed them? Could they shift for themselves? There are over two million slaves in the South. Suppose they were all manumitted? What would become of them? The Abolitionists say they could be transported to Africa and colonized. I don't think it could be done. I only know that slavery is a reality to which the nation must—and can—adjust. To me, other things matter more: American progress, expansion, prosperity." He paused again. "But I'm a northerner, sir, by ancestry, birth, training, and I could never conscientiously be a slaveholder or enjoy the money earned by slave labor."

"I see," said Colonel Martin. "Every man must hearken to his conscience. Let us forget all this, shall we?"

"Gladly!" said Douglas.

The next day, when the bridal couple had set out for Chicago, Colonel Martin wrote a codicil to his will, bequeathing the Mississippi plantation to Martha, though with a qualifying clause: "In giving to my dear daughter Martha full control of my slaves in Mississippi, I make one request. That is, if she leaves no children, to make provision before she dies to have all these Negroes, together with their increase, sent to Liberia, or some other colony in Africa. I would remind my dear daughter that her husband does not wish to own such property."

Douglas would hear nothing about this codicil until Colonel Martin's death many months later. But then he would do nothing to prevent his wife's inheritance of the plantation and its slaves.

As the war wore on, the people of the United States liked it less and less. There seemed slight doubt that Mexico would be vanquished, but the battles were costing thousands of American lives. The Whigs said it was a trumped-up war, a monstrous Democratic mistake—Polk's mistake. Polk himself was saying that he would not run for a second term as President.

"And how prudent of him!" jeered the Whigs. "A second term? He'd never get it. Polk's goose is cooked!"

In the Senate, Douglas was as vocal as he had been in the House, and continued to speak in defense of the war. The anticipated American victory would bring with it much new territory. Timid souls might view the gain as a complication, disturbing to the delicate, precarious balance between slave and free states. But Douglas was not afraid. The Constitution did not forbid slavery, or even allude to the system. Slavery would never be forced upon northern states that abhorred it. Nor would it be snatched away from southern states where it was necessary to the economy.

The Abolitionists, said Douglas, were extremists; they painted slavery in somber tints of brutality, misery: the whip with nine lashes, the Negro mother torn from her brood and "sold down the river," the fugitive fleeing from a cruel master. But was this all of it? No, Douglas had observed conditions in the South, had known kind masters and Negroes so contented with their lot that they sang as they toiled. Of course, there were southern extremists, too, and they must be shunned. Extremists of any type, anywhere, were a threat to national unity.

The war ended in September, 1847, with the capture of Mexico City, the Mexican capital, by American infantrymen and marines. The peace treaty, signed February 2, 1848, at Guadalupe Hidalgo, ceded to the United States all territory north of the Rio Grande and the Gila River, an area comprising the disputed strip of Texas, along with New Mexico, California, Nevada, Utah, Arizona and parts of Colorado and Wyoming.

Epochal though it was, the treaty came almost as an anticlimax to an earlier event. On January 28, at Johann Sutter's mill in Coloma, California, gold was discovered.

*Gold!* Like lightning, the word flashed north, south, east, over the ocean to Europe, and with corresponding speed thousands of treasure hunters scurried westward, traversing plains and deserts, scaling mountains, crossing the Isthmus of Panama, voyaging around Cape Horn—on, on, toward the glittering lure.

In this exciting period of treaty making and the gold rush, Senator Douglas was very busy. Every day stacked his desk with mail, much of it from Illinois.

"The homefolks seem to think I can do *anything,*" he once said. "They think I have Aladdin's lamp, a geni in a bottle."

He was asked to get jobs in Washington for Illinois Democrats, to file patent papers and affidavits for soldier's bounty, to write letters of introduction, to write articles for magazines. He was punctilious in answering all such appeals, generous with his time—and with his money. His investments in Chicago real estate, the "stake" he had bought years ago, had been wonderfully profitable. Now he could afford liberal donations to colleges and to artistic and cultural foundations. He never neglected the welfare of the "homefolks" or the opportunity to benefit the state. Learning that a Virginia mechanic, Cyrus H. McCormick, had invented a "machine known as the Virginia reaper," he interested a group of Chicago financiers in McCormick's machine, a contact that resulted in the formation of one of America's largest industrial plants.

His old Jacksonville friend, Murray McConnell, had a son who wanted to be a West Point cadet. McConnell's letter asking Senator Douglas to recommend "young George" for the military academy contained some local news.

"Our congressman is a Whig," McConnell wrote, "and rather a sorry specimens of even that low species."

The Whig congressman? That was Abraham Lincoln.

Yes, Lincoln had been elected to the House of Representatives in 1846. With his wife, Mary Todd Lincoln, and his little son Robert, he was now in Washington, ensconced in a rather drab boardinghouse on Capitol Hill. Lincoln was always in his seat when the roll of congressmen was called (a back seat, the poorest in the chamber); sometimes he was to be glimpsed, clad in his threadbare alpaca coat, at the Marine Band concerts, or bowling in an athletic gymnasium conveniently near the boardinghouse. He was a clumsy bowler; his scores were wretched, but his conversation was so refreshingly humorous that people collected in the gymnasium to listen and laugh with him.

To Springfield friends he had confessed that he was "scared" in Congress, as scared as he used to be trying cases in the Sangamon County Court. "But not *more* scared," he said. "As you all are so anxious for me to distinguish myself, I have concluded to do so."

And how had he distinguished himself?

He had voted against the Mexican War. There were things worth fighting for, but conquest, he thought, was not one of them. Soon after coming into the House, he made a speech branding the war as unrighteous, the ignoble attack of a strong nation on a weaker nation, and had asked President Polk to designate the spot where Mexicans had shed American blood on American soil. The "spot speech" aroused only a languid curiosity among the newspaper men reporting Congressional proceedings: "Who has the floor? Lincoln? And who the devil is Lincoln? Oh, that gawky Illinois rail splitter! What's he yowling about? Nothing, probably."

In his next speech he again assailed the President. Criticism of the sort was ordinarily publicized, but no notice was taken of this speech, either. The other Illinois representatives seemed oblivious to it; none of the eastern Whigs commented on it. President Polk kept a voluminous diary in which every night he recorded the doings of the previous day from breakfast to bedtime, a diary full of names; but not then or ever did Polk refer to Abraham Lincoln. Apparently the "gawky rail splitter" was unknown to the Chief Executive he had dared to challenge.

But Springfield heard about the "spot speech." Oh, yes, and the people in the town and district were hurt and resentful. They had not sent Abe Lincoln to Congress for this! Many Illinois boys and men had been killed, and more wounded, in Mexico. John Hardin, colonel of the state's militia and one of its best-loved sons, had fallen in the battle at Buena Vista; his body had been returned to Jacksonville for an elaborate funeral fraught with patriotic ardor. John Hardin and Lincoln had been old friends, comrades. Yet now Lincoln had the audacity to imply that Hardin and all the rest had sacrificed their lives for an unrighteous cause!

How strange and disillusioning it was! And what a contrast to the splendid behavior of Stephen Douglas, who spoke tenderly and reminiscently of Hardin, their friendship which political differences had not marred, their march to Nauvoo, their successful coping with the Mormons. Douglas, in the Senate, praised John Hardin; he praised and mourned for all the Illinois dead.

Lincoln had been bewildered by Springfield's reaction to the "spot speech." For the remainder of his term in the House, he raised his voice only to vote on measures that pertained to slavery. He was not an Abolitionist, but he felt that slavery must be restricted.

On February 26, 1848, the day of John Quincy Adams' burial, Lincoln and Douglas both walked in Old Man Eloquent's funeral procession, Lincoln with the representatives, Douglas with the senators. They both saw the laying of the cornerstone of the monument memorializing George Washington. That was July 4, 1848, a day of band music, waving flags, chiming church bells and thundering cannon. As the veterans of the Mexican War paraded through the city to the monument site, Douglas was on the platform among the great and famous of the country, Lincoln stood with the congressmen in front of the platform—where he was distinguished for his height and for nothing else.

On July 27, Lincoln made his last speech in Congress, endorsing General Zachary Taylor's nomination as the Whigs' Presidential candidate. Then he went home to Springfield. In his absence, his law practice had dwindled, he was hard up and in debt.

Taylor was elected in the autumn. With a Whig administration dispensing patronage, Lincoln sought the post of Illinois land commissioner, the job that once had been Douglas', but, somehow, he didn't get it. Springfield gossips said that he could have been appointed as the territorial governor of Oregon, but that his wife had told him she would never go to Oregon, never, it was too uncivilized a place.

"Mary Lincoln's foot may be small," the gossips said, "but she can put it down mighty firmly!"

Already the Democrats were looking forward to 1852.

"We'll elect a President of *our* party then," they said. "A western President, Douglas of Illinois."

Douglas himself was making no prognostications. He and Martha were in Washington, and rejoicing over the birth of their first child, a husky baby boy whom they named Robert Martin, for his maternal grandfather.

# 12

# "THE ETERNAL WORD"

"Slavery, slavery, is the eternal word in Congress," lamented a visitor to the Capitol in 1849. "Hell is to pay and no pitch hotter. It is appalling to hear gentlemen sworn to support the Constitution talk, and talk earnestly, for a dissolution of this Union."

But the talk was not confined to congressional precincts. As new territories were formed in the spacious regions gained by the Mexican War, the slavery question took precedence over everything else. The North and the South greedily grasped for power; public sentiment was fast becoming so divided that thoughtful citizens wondered whether the breach could ever be healed.

Stephen Douglas saw these portents, deplored them—and refused to be terrified by them. While his colleagues were at loggerheads about slavery, he was originating and pushing through the Senate bills to develop the West, the Mississippi Valley, to create railroads, modernize transportation, expand commerce and manufacturing. To him, a dissolution of the Union seemed as unlikely as the end of the world. Even the most serious dissensions—even the knotty problems relating to slavery—could all be ironed out, if only the people and their lawmakers were guided by common sense, not by passion.

California, quickly populated by the gold rush, now asked for

103

admittance to the Union as a free state, a petition that threw
Congress into a furore. In 1849 there were thirty states, fifteen
slave, fifteen free. The conferring of statehood upon California
would give the North an advantage for which the South must
somehow be compensated, or there might indeed be hell to pay!

In January, 1850, Senator Henry Clay of Kentucky devised a
plan that he believed would meet the emergency. Clay was
seventy-three years old; his life had been spent in political service, in the Kentucky legislature, in the House of Representatives,
as secretary of state, as senator. He was a Whig, but trusted by
many Americans outside of his own party. He had often been
a candidate for the Presidency, an office he coveted and was
never to reach. He was a slaveholder, but one who loved the
Union and wanted to see his country at peace.

Clay's plan, which came to be known as the Omnibus Bill,
was a compromise, though rather more favorable to the South
than to the North. Its provisions were fivefold: for the admittance of California as a free state; the prohibition of the slave
trade (but not slaveholding) in the District of Columbia; the
organization of Utah and New Mexico as territories with no
ban on slavery; the reclaiming from Texas, for ten million dollars, of a portion of New Mexico; the enactment of a new and
stringent fugitive slave law.

For months the Omnibus Bill was wrangled over in the Senate. Every day, Henry Clay spoke for it—against bitter opposition from the South as well as the North. John C. Calhoun,
the great man of South Carolina, would have none of it. Compromise? The South demanded complete equality with the
North, and no tampering with slavery anywhere!

Calhoun was ill with a disease from which he could not re-
cover. On the day that he was to speak against the Omnibus
Bill, he tottered into the Senate Chamber on the arm of Senator

James M. Mason of Virginia. Too feeble to stand, his voice failing, he huddled in his chair, grim and glaring, wrapped in flannels like a mummy, while his speech was read for him by Senator Mason.

" 'The cry of *Union, Union, the glorious Union* cannot avert disunion. It is as futile as if a physician should cry *Health, health, glorious health* when his patient lies at the door of death!' "

So Calhoun, at death's door himself, had written, and so he meant.

Clay and Calhoun were two of the Senate's three most eminent sages. Daniel Webster was the third. Webster, elderly and austere, had long been a foe of slavery, looked on by the Abolitionists as their friend. But on March 7, in a dramatic burst of oratory, Webster answered Calhoun, the secessionists, the Abolitionists and all factions thereof by declaring his approval of Clay's compromise: "I speak today not as a Massachusetts man, nor as a northern man, but as an American. I speak for the preservation of the Union. Hear me for my cause!"

As the weeks went by, other statesmen of lesser fame entered the controversy—and Stephen Douglas consulted with Clay. Douglas told Clay that his bill would never pass. The Omnibus, he said, must be overturned, its contents spilled out and disentangled, the five measures voted on separately.

Clay demurred. "A mammoth task! Who will assume it?"

"I will," Douglas said. "Let me!"

Through the spring and summer months he worked, making the single bill into five bills, bringing each one before the Congress and, when that one passed, going on to the next, thus securing the enacting of a historic compromise—the Compromise of 1850.

Henry Clay said gratefully that Douglas had accomplished

what seemed the impossible. Senator Jefferson Davis of Mississippi said, "If any man has a right to be proud at this time, it is Stephen A. Douglas of Illinois." And many people, both North and South, felt that only Douglas' foresight and energy had saved the country from civil war.

Douglas was not complacent. The Compromise, he thought, was not perfect, but it was expedient, it would be welcomed by all who wanted domestic concord.

"Now we can relax," he said, "and learn to live together without envy and selfishness. Now the West will have a chance to grow!"

When Congress adjourned, he went back to Chicago ("the finest city in America," he called it) to Martha and young Robert Martin Douglas, who soon would be celebrating his second birthday.

He arrived home on a chill autumn evening and was greeted by a fond but frightened wife.

"Oh, Stephen," said Martha, "everybody is so angry at you!"

"Angry? Why?"

"That new fugitive slave law! Chicago people hate it, they think the congressmen who voted for it are steeped in sin! And it's all your fault! They're having a protest meeting this very night."

Douglas had taken off his hat; he put it on again. "Where is the meeting?"

"But you're not going! No, no—"

"I must go," he said. "Don't worry, Martha. Nothing will happen to me."

The meeting was just ending when he walked into the hall and up the aisle to the stage. "My good friends and constituents—"

They eyed him glumly, someone hissed, someone shouted, "You're too late, Senator. Too late."

"It is late, I know. But will you come here tomorrow night? I have something to say to you." When there was no response, he smiled. "Well, anyway, *I'll* be here, waiting for you."

The next night the hall was full. Chicagoans were angry, but he was their Little Giant, they were accustomed to listening to him. Calmly, meticulously, as if presenting a case to a panel of judges, he elucidated the 1850 Compromise. He had rehearsed what he must say, especially about the fugitive slave law, which had been designed to appease the South. It provided that fugitive Negroes, if recaptured, could not be tried by a jury or testify in their own behalf, and levied heavy penalties on persons who aided or sheltered them.

His theme was obedience to the Constitution. It was natural, he said, that northerners should pity the Negro who escaped from bondage. It was natural that they should have an innate suspicion of slavery. But this new law, drastic as it might seem, conformed with the Constitution and had been duly passed by majorities in both the House and the Senate. To defy it, to set it at naught, would be to defy the Constitution:

"I am sure that Chicagoans have no such intention!"

"But what about *divine* law?" shouted a heckler. "Is slavery a law of God?"

"Divine law," he said, "does not prescribe the form of government under which we shall live, or the character of our political and civil institutions."

He was imperturbable, good-humored, and as they talked they softened. He had never deceived them. He was usually right. Who had the temerity to get up and say that he was wrong now? Nobody!

In 1852, at the national Democratic convention in Baltimore, Douglas was a strong contender for the Presidential nomination. For a week the delegates bickered and balloted, and then chose Franklin Pierce of New Hampshire. If Douglas was chagrined, he did not show it. He wanted to be President, and said as much to his friends. But he was only thirty-nine, there was still time for it. He congratulated Mr. Pierce and helped to elect him in November.

And he knew himself to be a very lucky man, a happy man. His business ventures were lucrative, his health was excellent, his reputation was enhanced with the years. He had been re-elected to the Senate. Colleges had given him honorary degrees; he was a director in scientific societies in Illinois, Washington and New York, a patron of education and the arts. He had bought an estate, Oakenwald, in Chicago, eighty acres of lake shore forest on which he meant to build a fine big house.

His family life was without flaw. He and Martha were now the parents of a second son, whom they had named Stephen Arnold Douglas, Jr. He was an indulgent father to the two boys, never too busy to romp and play with them. His ties with his mother were as close as ever they had been, and he went often to see her. His affectionate relationship with Sarah seemed to deepen with the years; when Sarah's husband, Julius Granger, died, it was to her brother that she turned for advice and consolation.

Until 1853, Douglas' only brush with grief had been the death of Julius Granger. Then, suddenly, his whole world seemed to shatter into bits. Martha died in childbirth and the baby, a little daughter, lived but a few hours longer.

These terrible losses plunged him into an abyss of despair from which, it seemed, he could not rise. His nights were sleepless, he ate almost nothing. Shut into his library, he slouched at his desk, surly and unshaven, and would not be comforted.

His doctor took him in hand. "Senator," the doctor said, "for the sake of your boys, you must pick up the threads of existence."

"Yes, yes, I know," he said. "But how can I? What am I to do?"

"You must find some diversion. Travel, a change of scene. You have never gone abroad. Go to Europe."

"And leave the boys? With whom?"

"You have a widowed sister, haven't you? Leave them with her."

Sarah? He thought about it, and wrote to her: "Dear Sarah, will you come? Would it be too great an imposition?"

Of course Sarah would come! She read his letter and came on the next train. She hugged Douglas, hugged and petted the boys.

"Imposition?" she said. "After all you've done for me? Go on to Europe, Stephen. Don't fret about a thing here. Just get well and strong again, and like yourself."

She looked over the house and said, "You have eleven servants. That's too many! A cook, a butler, maids, a coachman, grooms, gardeners—why, it's scandalous! I shall dismiss them all."

He remonstrated. "Servants are a necessity, Sarah."

"I'll dismiss them and then hire back those I need."

"But—I don't understand."

"It will make them know that I'm their employer while you're away."

Despite his sadness, Douglas laughed.

His first stop in Europe was at London. At the time of the Oregon dispute he had spoken harshly of England, and now the British were rather cool to him. But because he was a senator, they did not wish to alienate him. Therefore, an emissary of the British government called on him at his hotel and said that he could be introduced to Queen Victoria.

"The court costume, Senator Douglas, is knee breeches, silk stockings, buckled slippers and a sword," the emissary said.

He smiled and shook his head. "I shall be pleased to meet Her Majesty—in my ordinary attire, sir."

"No, no! That would not be proper," said the emissary.

"I think it would. In my country, foreign visitors are introduced to our President in the regalia of whatever rank they have at home. I wear my frock coat at the White House, I shall wear it at Buckingham Palace."

The emissary frowned. "At least, Senator, you will wear a short sword? You really must!"

"A sword? With my frock coat? No," he said. "And perhaps it would be best for me not to meet the Queen at all."

From London, where he did not meet the Queen, he traveled on to the continent of Europe, where he saw much that interested him. In Genoa, Italy, he made a sketch of the harbor breakwater, thinking that a structure of the sort could be built to widen the harbor at Chicago. In Germany, he studied the Prussian tariff regulations; they might be of use, he felt, in the United States also. In Russia, he rented a droshka and drove over the steppes; they were not unlike the Illinois prairies, he said. In St. Petersburg, he was welcomed with flattering courtesy, rode on a prancing steed to review the imperial troops and (wearing his frock coat) dined with the Czar. In France, he was feted by the Emperor Louis Napoleon and the beautiful Empress Eugénie.

"What a delightful man, this Mr. Stephen Douglas," said Eugénie. "How gallantly he bows!"

In October, loaded down with presents for his boys and Sarah, he sailed for home. He disembarked at New York and was besieged by newspaper reporters.

"Well, how are you, Senator?" they asked. "How was your trip?"

"It was a good trip. I am rested, physically and mentally," he said.

"And what did you think of Europe?"

"Europe has its good points."

"Would you want to live there?"

"Never," he answered. "Never! I wouldn't swap one square mile of Chicago for the whole of Europe—including the British Isles."

The reporters chuckled. "Douglas is still Douglas," they said. "Still American and western to the core."

In Chicago, the boys fell upon him with cries of rapture, and Sarah gave him a hearty kiss.

"You know, Stephen," Sarah said, "I like it here. I think I'll stay with you for a few months."

"For as long as you will, Sarah," he said. "Please do!"

# 13

# THE KANSAS-NEBRASKA BILL

Douglas' political allies had supposed that he would run for the Presidency in 1856, but shortly after his return from Europe he told them that he would not be a candidate for the Democratic nomination.

"Let us not think of that now," he said. "Our first duty is to the cause."

The cause? A new cause?

Yes, Senator Douglas meant to organize the territory of Nebraska. Immediately, and against any and all opposition!

Though astonished, his friends saw this sudden move as consistent with his determination to develop the West. He did not reveal to them that he had also in mind the establishment of a great railroad route which would have Chicago as its eastern terminus and span the continent to the Pacific coast.

To Douglas himself the idea was not new. From the very beginning of his career, he had been the railroads' stanchest champion. In the Illinois legislature, in the House of Representatives and the Senate, he had exerted his influence for the granting of public lands on which to lay the shining steel tracks. For several years he had been ready to put forward his scheme of a transcontinental route, and had waited only until a way could be cleared for it.

But now he found that southern statesmen had a scheme of

their own. They, too, wanted a great railroad—one that would miss Chicago by hundreds of miles and have the city of Memphis as its eastern terminus. And there was no unopened territory blocking the southern route. If Douglas wished, as he did, to make Chicago the metropolis of the North, he would have to act at once!

On January 4, 1854, he brought before the Senate a bill for the organization of Nebraska, and on January 23, offered a substitute bill which would divide the area into two tracts, Nebraska and Kansas. Both bills incorporated "squatter" or "popular sovereignty," the right of the inhabitants to legislate for or against slavery as it pleased them. The first bill implied a repeal of the Missouri Compromise of 1820. The second would entirely repeal the old compromise.

If Senator Douglas had exploded a carload of dynamite in the Capitol, the effect could not have been more shocking. Instantly, the uneasy truce between the North and the South, prevailing since 1850, was shattered, and northerners were in an uproar. Those citizens who detested slavery had thought of the Missouri Compromise as an anchor to which all their hopes of restricting the system were moored. Now Stephen Douglas, alone and singlehanded, without previous agitation or notice, was trying to set it aside, to provide for the spread of slavery onto soil long consecrated to freedom!

And was not this the same Douglas who, nine years ago, in the House, had urged the maintenance of the Missouri Compromise line?

What had come over him? What was the reason for his face-about? What *could* be his reason?

In the North a variety of sinister accusations were hurled at him. It was said that he wanted to be President—and so avidly that he would betray the people who loved and trusted him. His bill was nothing but a bid for southern votes. He was the blind tool of the South, a pawn of the slaveholders. Yes, and a slaveholder himself, a northern absentee landlord, with a plantation in Mississippi, whereon coffles of Negroes drudged wearily in clanking chains!

Not then or in the following weeks did he speak of his railroad project, his vision of Chicago's future. Had he done so, he might have been spared some of the tirades. In every antislavery community there were mass meetings to denounce him. Ministers of all denominations in a thousand pulpits inveighed against him. Newspapers, particularly the Abolitionist press, bristled with virulent editorials, petitions for the defeat of his bill showered like hail upon congressmen. Dummies of straw and cloth were labeled "Douglas," doused in oil, strung up on lampposts and set afire.

He was to say later, "I could have traveled from Boston to Chicago by the light of my flaming effigies."

Much of the antagonism he had expected and braced himself to endure stoically—but not all. Occasionally he was goaded to hit out at his maligners. He wrote to an eastern minister that he had never shaped his conduct in public affairs for his personal enrichment: "Examine my record! I do not shrink from the scrutiny." To another, he denied that he was or had ever been a slaveholder: "That Mississippi plantation belonged to my wife and is now the property of my young sons, in accordance with a will of which I was the executor. The Negroes there do not go in chains . . . I have no desire to be better or purer in heart than such slaveholders."

To the anonymous letters, dozens of them, which said that the death of his wife had been Almighty God's punishment for his wickedness, he did not reply.

One evening he went into the Brown Hotel in Washington

to talk with George McConnell, the young man from Jacksonville whom he had recommended as a West Point cadet. On the table in George's room was a copy of the *National Era,* an Abolitionist publication. Douglas had been smiling, but as he glanced at the paper he sighed.

"This article, 'The Appeal of the Independent Democrats.' You read it, George? I dare say everybody in town has read that my bill is a devilish plot and I'm an archcriminal."

"Charles Sumner and Salmon Chase wrote it, didn't they, sir?" said George.

"Yes, and other senators. They asked for a postponement on the voting, so that they could 'digest' the bill. I agreed, and they have utilized the time to set the Abolitionists on me." Douglas took a cigar from his pocket and paced back and forth on the hearth rug. "My boy, never go into politics. If you do, however sincerely you may work for the good of your country—the *whole* country—you will be misunderstood, misquoted, traduced and finally sacrificed on the altar of avarice and egotism. Adams, Webster and Henry Clay were victims; I am marked to be the next."

As George McConnell said nothing, Douglas went on: "Slavery! It's a curse to white men as well as black. But the only thing that can eliminate it is the sword, and if that is ever resorted to, then no one can foretell the end. I would not violate the Constitution to destroy slavery, or for any purpose. The Union is worth more to humanity than any race, black or white!"

Flinging his cigar into the grate fire, he paced again. "The repeal of the Missouri Compromise is a step toward freedom. Why can't these northern Democrats see that? Do away with that old line and slavery can no longer crouch behind it—a line which freedom cannot cross. Yet even in my own party, I'm called a traitor." He paused, pounded the table with his fist. "*They* are the traitors, George! A storm is brewing, we may all be engulfed in it. But I love the United States—and I'll stick to the old ship while there's a plank of her afloat!"

He would stick to his bill, too. The Little Giant had on his "fighting clothes."

In the Senate, the debating dragged on for days and weeks. The foes of the Kansas-Nebraska Bill were allotted ample time in which to rip it to shreds and expose its alleged fallacies. As chairman of the sponsoring committee, Douglas would have the last word.

At eleven o'clock of a raw, damp March night, his turn came. The galleries of the chamber were packed; the statesmen below were alert, flurried.

Douglas got to his feet. The chairman recognized him: "Senator Douglas?"

Poised and as always well-groomed, his black hair brushed back from his forehead, blue eyes glinting, he said: "Since the hour is very late and the argument has been so lengthy, I shall waive the privilege of speaking and ask that the Kansas-Nebraska Bill be voted upon without further delay."

But cries sounded from the floor, the galleries: "No, no! Speak!"

So he spoke—and never more forcefully. Other orators had been impressive; Douglas was masterful, swaying this audience as he had swayed many like it. Even his political adversaries were grudgingly admiring. The most ruthless of them, Senator William Seward of New York, was heard to mutter: "I've never had so much respect for him as I have tonight."

The Missouri Compromise? He said that once he had thought

it must be kept as the boundary between free soil and slave, and extended through Texas and all the territories to the Pacific coast. But conditions had changed. The Missouri Compromise had been superseded by the measures enacted in 1850; now it would not suffice to the nation's needs. Like all outmoded things, the Missouri Compromise must be discarded.

As for slavery, climate and geography would limit it; there was no danger of slavery's invading where it was not wanted. But in this, and in every governmental matter, the will of the people must be the deciding factor. Popular sovereignty was the only true self-government. Let the voice of the people rule!

At five o'clock, as the night merged slowly into a wet gray dawn, the vote was taken. By a majority of twenty-three the Senate passed the Kansas-Nebraska Bill.

Douglas had worked hard for his victory; he was pleased when, in May, the bill was passed in the House of Representatives and signed by President Pierce, thus becoming a federal statute. But he knew that it had yet to be "sold" to the country at large. Vast numbers of northerners still chafed at the severity of the 1850 fugitive slave law and felt that now insult had been added to injury. Many of them were inclining toward Abolitionism. And many more were reading an extraordinary, disturbing novel—*Uncle Tom's Cabin*.

Three hundred thousand copies of this book by Harriet Beecher Stowe were bought in the first twelve months after its publication. Translated into twenty different languages, it was exported abroad for foreign consumption; eventually it would encircle the globe. Mrs. Stowe, an Ohio housewife, had little knowledge of slaves or slavery, but she knew that the institution was an evil that no sophistry, no amount of subtle rationalizing, no law could mitigate. Her book was fanciful, her literary style effusive, but she wrote with a trenchant pen, endowing her Little Eva, Topsy and Uncle Tom with a haunting pathos.

Far more than she could ever have dreamed, Harriet Beecher Stowe's pen had hastened a national crisis.

In politics, the year was one of confusion, with parties being unmade and remade. The Whigs were disintegrating, the Democrats splitting into factions. The Know-Nothing party, based on religious and racial intolerance, was born and grew stealthily, and another new party was forming: the Republican party, composed of dissident Whigs and rebellious Democrats, all of them pledged to fight slavery on every front.

When Douglas left Washington for Illinois he was confident that he could "sell" the Kansas-Nebraska Bill to the people at home. But the journey westward was disconcerting. From the train windows he saw scarecrows that were caricatures of himself displayed in fields and fence corners. At a stop in one Ohio village, a group of women pounced upon him, wailing *"Judas, Judas!"* and pelting him with thirty silver coins. Arrived in Chicago, he found the newspapers depicting him in hideous cartoons. He was told that if he endeavored to "vindicate his crimes" he would arouse "the lion" he could not tame.

Undaunted, he said that on Saturday evening, September 1, he would address his fellow citizens from the balcony of a downtown building.

That was a hot night in Chicago, hot and strangely quiet. During the day, the city had seemed to be in mourning, with flags lowered to half-mast and church bells tolling funeral dirges. At twilight the tolling ceased. Men and women, some of them armed with clubs, or with slingshots and sacks of pebbles, seeped into the streets and massed around the building where Douglas was to speak. There was no noise. As mute as if molded in wax, they waited.

He came in his carriage. He got out and ascended to the balcony.

"My friends, I am here to say to you—"

Then catcalls, groans and hoots burst forth.

"My friends—"

The din increased to bedlam, ribald chanting and obscene taunts.

He shrugged. "Well, I'm not in a hurry—"

But when he had faced them for four hours and it was after midnight and still they chanted and shouted, he cried abruptly, angrily: "Abolitionists of Chicago, it is now Sunday morning! I am going to church—and you may go to hell!"

They swarmed behind him as he climbed back into his carriage. His coachman flicked the whip; the horses pulled sharply away from the curb. A barrage of rocks flew; the horses reared. A woman shrieked hysterically, "Kill him! Douglas, the little bully of slavery!"

The coachman trembled. "They're a gang o' hoodlums, Senator."

"Yes," he said. "But they'll simmer down. Drive on."

"And what—what'll you do now, sir?"

"Do? I shall speak all over the state for the Kansas-Nebraska Bill," he said.

He started that very week, going from town to town, always drawing a crowd and usually abuse, from which he did not flinch. And soon he discovered that someone else was traveling the same course—an old acquaintance, Abraham Lincoln of Springfield.

Lincoln had recently identified himself with the new Republican party. In his dingy Springfield law office, he had studied the congressional debates dealing with the repeal of the Missouri Compromise. He had studied Douglas' bill. In the summer, while Douglas was still in the East, Lincoln had been out on the stump in Illinois, speaking against the bill. He had come to a conclusion which he would repeat many times, from which he never afterward would swerve:

*This nation cannot exist half slave and half free.*

Lincoln crossed Douglas' path at Bloomington. Rather diffidently, he entered the hotel suite where the Little Giant was receiving visitors.

Douglas was cordial. "Well, Mr. Lincoln, I'm glad to see you!"

They shook hands, but Lincoln seemed shy, lingering for only a moment of aimless conversation. An hour later a Bloomington Republican who was a friend of his came to Douglas, "Perhaps you wondered, Senator, why Lincoln called on you," said the friend.

Douglas laughed. "Yes, I did. He was a fish out of water here."

"He wanted to ask whether he could share the platform with you tonight, but his nerve failed him. I am his emissary. What do you say?"

Somehow Douglas was irked by the request. "No," he answered. "Mr. Lincoln will have to arrange his own speaking schedule."

Douglas did not remain for Lincoln's Bloomington meeting; he went on to Springfield—and found Mr. Lincoln in the hotel lobby, announcing that on the next afternoon, he would reply to Senator Douglas.

"He's trailing me," Douglas said to the Springfield Democratic committee. "The fellow is shadowing me."

This time Douglas stayed to hear Lincoln. Amiably smiling,

he sat in the front row. Lincoln, on the rostrum, was coatless, his shirt wrinkled, his boots muddy. He spoke in thin, rasping tones, his gaunt countenance quivering with feeling.

Slavery, Lincoln said, must not be allowed to reach into the new western lands, the Missouri Compromise should never have been repealed. "Senator Douglas has told you that the white residents in any territory are good enough to govern themselves and therefore good enough to govern a few miserable Negroes. *I* tell you no man is good enough to govern another man without that other's consent!"

As Lincoln finished, Douglas got up and delivered an impromptu talk, refuting all that Lincoln had said—and was gratified by the crowd's enthusiastic applause. But his annoyance returned when Lincoln followed him to Peoria and he was informed that Old Abe had vowed to "run him into his hole and make him holler 'Quits!'"

Never disposed to such "hollering," he went on through the central and southern counties of the state, and now his tour was less turbulent. This was Douglas' old stamping ground; he knew every mile of it. These people were not antislavery zealots; they listened attentively as he expounded the merits of the Kansas-Nebraska Bill and cheered loudly for their Little Giant. He went into Indiana and Ohio, then swung back toward Chicago.

At home once more, he thought the outlook was much brighter. The hoodlums had, indeed, simmered down and a great many Chicagoans, though not all, were willing to believe that the bill was sensible and fair. When a public dinner was given in his honor, Douglas' serenity was restored.

"Our citizens will see that this legislation brings an end to sectional strife," he said. "If things go well on the western plains, we shall have an era of peace and progress."

# 14

# STORM IN THE WEST

Douglas' optimism about the western plains was premature. Things did not go well there; in 1855 they were going very badly. No sooner had his bill been passed than proslavery settlers, calling themselves the Sons of the South, scurried into Kansas, whereupon the Emigrant Aid Society, a group of New England Abolitionists, encouraged and financed as large an influx of free-soil homesteaders.

By the most flagrant and adept cheating at the polls, the Sons of the South won the first territorial elections and organized a proslavery legislature at Lecompton, to which President Pierce gave his tacit approval. Not to be outdone, the Free-Soilers then established their own governing body at Topeka—and a blood feud was loosed.

Slave partisans sacked and burned the free-soil town of Lawrence. In retaliation John Brown, a fanatic Abolitionist, with a band of seven antislavery stalwarts, raided and massacred five Sons of the South in their log huts on Pottawatomie Creek. Each day saw new thefts, plunderings and murders, and federal troops sent in by Pierce could not quell the forays.

In March, 1856, the Kansans at Topeka sought to have the territory taken into the Union as a free state. This precipitated a congressional struggle more bitter than any that had ever preceded it. All the latent fears and vicious hatreds of northern and southern radicals were unveiled. Senator Charles Sumner of Massachusetts made a scathing speech, "The Crime Against Kansas," in which he maliciously flayed several of his southern colleagues—among them, Senator Andrew P. Butler of South Carolina. Three days later Butler's nephew, young Preston Brooks, a congressman from South Carolina, waylaid Sumner in the Senate chamber, struck him down with a cane and whipped him until he lost consciousness, an incident so reprehensible that the whole country was appalled.

Douglas had been angered by Sumner's slandering of Andrew Butler. "Is it the object of the senator from Massachusetts to provoke some of us to kick him as we would a dog in the streets?" he had queried. But he was quick to say that Preston Brooks's reaction had been that of a barbarian and was not to be condoned.

He said also that extremists in both the North and the South were to blame for all such clashes, in Congress and in Kansas. The Emigrant Aid Society, he thought, was the prime offender.

When the session adjourned Kansas was still a territory. It was again the year for Presidential nominations. At the Democratic convention in Cincinnati, Douglas' name was placed before the delegates. As in 1852, the balloting was prolonged, with Douglas and James Buchanan of Pennsylvania the main contenders. Douglas had not gone to the convention; he was in Washington. After the sixteenth roll call, he telegraphed to those delegates who were stubbornly standing for him that he wished to withdraw from the race. Party solidarity meant everything to him: "We must hold to our Democratic principles!"

Buchanan was nominated on the seventeenth ballot, but many of the delegates were regretful. Threading through the cheers for the Pennsylvanian were dissonant voices crying, "Hurrah for Douglas, the Little Giant!"

A Washington reporter asked Douglas whether he would campaign for Buchanan.

"Of course," he said. "Did you think I would sulk in my tent? I'll do the best I can for him. Mr. Buchanan and I are in complete harmony on all issues."

"Mr. Buchanan is for popular sovereignty?"

"Oh, yes!"

"Will you run for the Democratic nomination in 1860, Senator?"

He smiled. "That will be for my party to say."

"But you'll surely run for re-election to the Senate in '58?"

"I think my Illinois friends will want me to."

"This new party—the Republicans—will probably have a candidate. Do you know who it'll be?"

"No," Douglas said. "I wonder."

The reporter scribbled away at his notes. He liked Stephen Douglas, as most journalists did. "Senator, I'm going to write a story about you for my paper. *Another* story, a big one. Anything you do or say is of interest to our readers. For instance, your hobbies?"

"Hobbies? Well, they are the exploration of the country's natural resources, the education of our young people."

"And the development of the West?"

"Yes. That, especially."

"You're a regent of the Smithsonian Institution, aren't you? And haven't you deeded your Oakenwald estate as the site for a college in Chicago?"

"Some of it," Douglas corrected, "for a *university*—Chicago University. I have the honor of being president of the board of trustees. We're raising a building fund and have employed an architect. The blueprints are in my office now."

The reporter folded his notes. "I'll send you a copy of my story, sir."

"Yes, do," Douglas said. "I shall want to see how I come off in it, for good or ill."

Buchanan was elected in November, but his majority was not large. Several normally Democratic states had slid over into the Republican column, and for the first time in history an avowed antislavery candidate, John C. Frémont, had polled a substantial vote. Thousands of northern Democrats were beginning to be skeptical of popular sovereignty: it hadn't soothed the wounds of "bleeding Kansas"; they thought it never would. These Democrats had not relished Franklin Pierce's southern bias. They waited dourly to see what Buchanan's attitude would be.

On Thanksgiving Day, 1856, Douglas married Miss Adele Cutts, a beautiful and intelligent Washington girl. Adele was a grandniece of the legendary Dolley Madison, who as President James Madison's wife and then his widow, had for so long dominated the capital's social circles. Adele's grandfather had been a congressman, her father was an official in the government's Treasury Department.

Though she was twenty years younger than Douglas, Adele had known and admired him for a long time. Where had they first met? Neither of them could remember.

"It may have been when I made my debut," she said. "But even before that, I knew Stephen. We have so many of the same friends, we believe in the same things—and I used to go to hear him speak in the Senate chamber."

For their wedding trip, Douglas and Adele went to visit his mother and Sarah. Back in Washington for the Christmas season, they moved into a spacious house in Minnesota Row.

Douglas was very proud of his young wife, and his small sons adored her. She had always been a favorite in Washington society. Now she was a charming hostess, setting new styles for entertaining.

At her Saturday afternoon teas, she draped curtains over the windows and lighted the house from top to bottom with candles. Her guests gasped. Candlelight by day? What an innovation! But how lovely it was, and how clever of Adele to think of it! Soon candlelight by day was all the vogue.

Douglas enjoyed the conviviality that had been brought into his house. He liked Adele's dinners and balls, liked having people around him. It pleased him to know that invitations to the Douglases' were much prized.

One night, a guest at their elegant dinner table said to him: "Senator, I'm told that you were once a cabinetmaker."

"I was," he said. "Yes, as a boy in Vermont I made cabinets and bureaus, lots of them—and good ones."

"And you are still a cabinetmaker."

"Am I?"

"Of course," the guest said. "Look about you. Most of the men here owe their positions to you."

He was amused. "But am I still a *good* cabinetmaker? It's being expert at your job that counts."

Douglas, the cabinetmaker. He was often to think of that epithet, always with a smile. He was stouter now, more florid in complexion, his thick hair graying becomingly at the temples. When the Washington reporter's story was printed in the newspaper, Douglas read it and afterward his son Robert read it aloud to him.

Robert was just learning to read; slowly and carefully he spelled out the sentences . . . "This little man, the famous politician of the West, has done more in the last four years than any other man in North America, more even than the President, to give direction to public affairs . . . He is the Little Giant, Stephen A. Douglas. . . ."

"But why do they say you're *little*, Father?" Robert asked.

"Because, Robert, every man and his destiny are little, as compared with the destiny of his country—though politicians of all sizes are prone to forget the fact."

"Oh?" said Robert. "Do you sometimes forget it?"

"No," he said. "I never have and I never will."

Buchanan was inaugurated on March 4, 1857, and on March 6, before the flowers adorning the inaugural ceremonies had wilted in their vases, the United States Supreme Court rendered a decision in the case of Dred Scott *vs.* Sandford. The case was of vital significance; the decision aggravated the nation's tension and chilled antislavery partisans to the very marrow of their bones.

Dred Scott was a slave who had been taken by his white master, an army surgeon, from the slave state of Missouri into Illinois, where slavery had been banned by the old Ordinance of 1787, and from there into Wisconsin, a free state by virtue of the Missouri Compromise. Returned to Missouri, Scott had sued for his liberty, alleging that residence in the free North had made him a free man. Since 1846 the case had dragged through the Missouri state courts and the federal district court.

Now, finally, Chief Justice Roger Taney of the Supreme Court handed down an opinion from which there could be no further appeal.

The opinion was very definite, very succinct. Dred Scott, said Chief Justice Taney, was not a citizen of the United States "within the meaning of the Constitution." He could not be a citizen, nor could his children be citizens. The Missouri Compromise to which he had looked for redress was unconstitutional. Dred Scott was a Negro "held to service or labor." And, going further, Chief Justice Taney said that Dred Scott had not even the right, constitutionally, to file a suit in a federal court.

When this decision was made known to the country at large, northerners were utterly dismayed. It set the seal of death on the Missouri Compromise. It seemed to wipe out all hope that slavery could be prohibited in any of the western territories. And wasn't it also a deathblow to Senator Douglas' cherished theory of popular sovereignty?

"No," said Douglas. "No, it is not!"

In June he went to Springfield to tell the Illinois General Assembly that the Dred Scott Decision did not invalidate popular sovereignty. He had thought his audience in the statehouse would be small, composed only of the legislators, but he found that everybody in town wanted to hear him. He saw Abraham Lincoln in the crowd.

"Good evening, Mr. Lincoln," he said, bowing.

Lincoln smiled. "How are you, Judge?"

Other people might call Stephen Douglas "Senator," but to Abraham Lincoln, he was always "Judge."

The burden of Douglas' speech was that the province of the Supreme Court was to interpret the Constitution, that in the case of Dred Scott the Court had not erred in its interpretation. Nor was the ruling incompatible with popular sovereignty. The separate states would retain all their legislative prerogatives; they could permit, limit or forbid slavery as their separate needs dictated.

"To resist the Dred Scott Decision," he said, "would be to imperil the Union."

He spoke of racial equality. The Abolitionists preached that the Negro was entitled to all the rights of the white man. But

Douglas believed, as did Chief Justice Taney and a majority of the associate justices, that the Negro could never be classed as a citizen. In every age, Negroes had shown themselves as incapable of self-government, requiring the wise, understanding and humane control of white men.

From Springfield, Douglas went back to Washington. Though somewhat extemporaneous, his speech had been eloquent. It was widely quoted, and reproduced in a brochure for national distribution.

Two weeks later, in the same place, Abraham Lincoln spoke, telling the same people that slavery was wrong, that the Dred Scott Decision was wrong, that popular sovereignty could no more stem the tide of slavery than a leaky dike can check a ruinous flood—that in his right to eat the bread earned with his own hands, the Negro was the white man's equal, Abraham Lincoln's equal, the equal of all other men.

During the following months, Douglas in Washington was concerned about Kansas, where confusion waxed rather than waned. In the territorial elections of October, 1857, the Kansas Free-Soilers outnumbered the proslavery settlers by three to one, which would seem to mean that when Kansas entered the Union, it would be a free state. But southern agents had conspired with the proslavery legislature at Lecompton and drawn up a state constitution so ambiguously phrased that whoever voted for statehood would have to vote for slavery. Therefore, in the next elections, many Free-Soilers abstained from voting at all. The southern partisans then passed the Lecompton constitution and in January, 1858, offered it to Congress for ratification.

The territorial governor of Kansas, Robert J. Walker, was a friend of Douglas'. He kept Douglas apprised of the deteriorating situation. Douglas felt a responsibility not only to Walker but to the law-abiding contingent of Kansas people. He felt that it was his duty to see that they were dealt with fairly. The Lecompton constitution was obviously a piece of cunning trickery; it must not be ratified.

And what of these rumors, as yet only whispered, that President Buchanan was aware of the trickery and did not protest it?

Douglas went to the White House, talked with the President —and realized that the rumors were not mere fabrications. Buchanan had weakly yielded to pressures put upon him by aggressive southern leaders; he would not oppose the Lecompton constitution.

For a moment Douglas was incredulous; then he said: "Mr. President, I have had faith in you. I have supported you. But if this is to be the administration's policy, I shall fight it to the last ditch."

Buchanan flushed and rose from his chair. He was a tall man, he towered above the Little Giant. "Mr. Douglas, let me remind you that no Democrat ever yet fought the policies of his own party's President without being crushed."

"You do not frighten me, sir," Douglas said coldly. "You did not elect me to the Senate. I am accountable to my constituency in Illinois, to my conscience and to God, but not to any President, or any other power on earth. The very essence of popular sovereignty is that no law shall be forced upon a people contrary to their wishes. The people of Kansas do not want a slave state. If given a choice, they would overwhelmingly reject the Lecompton constitution as a worthless and fraudulent scrap of paper. They must have that choice."

"So now you are an antislavery man, Mr. Douglas," said Buchanan.

"No," he said. "I am neither for nor against slavery. But I am against this gross deception. I will fight you to the last ditch. The Lecompton constitution will never be ratified."

Through the spring of 1858, Douglas fought Buchanan, many northern Democrats in Congress, all the South and most of the newspapers in the country. He knew that he was breaking with his party, and this distressed him sorely, for the party had been as dear to him as a religion. But he could not feel that he had deserted his Democratic ideals. Buchanan was the deserter, he thought.

"I'm just where I've always been," he said. "Where Andrew Jackson would have been—on the side of the people. And if I must hold the fort alone, I can and will."

Steered by the President, the Senate ratified the Lecompton constitution, with Douglas one of four Democrats voting in the negative. But in the House of Representatives opposition to the measure was heavier; there it was tossed from committee to committee and at length pigeonholed. In April an amended version of it was carried in both the Senate and the House.

But this, said Douglas, was not the last ditch! No, the amended state constitution had yet to be submitted to the voters of Kansas for their assent or rejection. Douglas had used every ounce of his influence to make sure that this time the polling should be sternly supervised, the voting legally conducted. He believed that the Kansans would reject a document which was at most a poor compromise.

Illinois Republicans had gleefully watched Douglas' tussle with Buchanan. It was the year when he would run for re-election to the Senate—the year to beat him, with the President and many members of his own party conniving in the beating!

At their state convention, the Republicans nominated a senatorial candidate who had no national prestige, such as the Little Giant's, but was pretty well known in Illinois. Accepting the nomination, the Republican candidate had said something that he was often to reiterate, something memorable: " 'A house divided against itself cannot stand.' I believe this government cannot endure permanently half slave and half free. I do not expect the Union to be dissolved—I do not expect the house to fall—but I do expect it will cease to be divided. It will become all one thing, or all the other."

When Douglas learned who was to be his rival, he smiled ruefully. "Abraham Lincoln is the strong man of his party," he said, "as honest as he is shrewd and the best stump speaker in the West. It will not be an easy chore to defeat Lincoln."

# 15

# TWO CANDIDATES

The interest of millions of Americans focused on Douglas as he started his political campaign in the summer of 1858. Since it was the function of the state legislatures to elect the United States senators, he would actually be campaigning for the election of Illinois legislative candidates running on the Democratic ticket. In order to win a third term in the Senate, Douglas must persuade the voters in all the Illinois towns and villages to send Democrats to the General Assembly in the autumn. If the majority in the Assembly was Democratic, then Douglas would retain his place in the Senate.

Eastern and Ohio newspapers said that the odds were against Douglas, he had alienated President Buchanan and disrupted his party, he was in "desperate straits." A Pennsylvania journalist said that in the past the Little Giant had evinced a genius for knocking down or leaping over any obstacles that hampered him, his name had been synonymous with success—but now he was risking everything he had attained.

Republican editors without exception said that "the wee Napoleon" was nearing his Waterloo.

Adele was to accompany her husband to Illinois. Douglas' advisers felt that her beauty and grace would be an asset to him, and she was eager to go.

"It will be an adventure," she said.

133

Her Washington society friends were somewhat supercilious. "A *rural* adventure," they remarked. "Well, you'll not have to worry about clothes. You can wear any old thing."

"No," said Adele. "Those are Stephen's people and, therefore, mine. I must look my best for them."

The Douglases took a roundabout route, first visiting the Granger relatives in Canandaigua and spending a few days in New York City. As they traveled west from New York, Douglas thought of the horrid effigies of himself that had disheartened him on his way home in 1854. But now at stations where the train stopped, there were crowds of friendly Democrats to shake his hand and wish him luck. Perhaps his straits were not so desperate as they had been described.

It was July 9 when he arrived in Chicago. As he alighted from the train, a battery of cannon saluted him. With Adele he got into an open barouche drawn by six white horses that whisked them through streets bright with bunting and pennants. In front of their hotel, the Tremont House, a huge transparency blazed a greeting:

*Welcome to Stephen A. Douglas*
THE DEFENDER OF POPULAR SOVEREIGNTY

As they stepped from the carriage, a squad of militiamen presented arms and thirty thousand Chicagoans shouted and applauded.

"Oh, Stephen, they *are* your people!" Adele exclaimed. "They really are!"

He had not intended to speak, but the cries of "Speech! Speech!" would not be silenced. Touched by such enthusiasm, he went out on the hotel balcony and spoke for almost an hour—about the "Kansas fraud" and why he had so obstinately fought it, about his Republican opponent's assertion that the country must be all slave or all free.

"I do not acknowledge that the Negro must have civil and political rights everywhere or nowhere," he said. "Mr. Lincoln, that worthy and honorable gentleman, is for uniformity in our domestic institutions, a uniformity which would lead to a war of sections until one or the other should be subdued. I am for the principle of the Kansas-Nebraska Bill, the right of the people to decide the slavery question, and all questions, for themselves."

The crowd did not want to let him go. When, tired and hoarse, he retreated to his suite, firecrackers were exploded, rockets shedding tails of sparks shot upward, and a brass band played "Yankee Doodle" under his windows.

A reporter for one of the Chicago papers saw Abraham Lincoln in the hotel lobby.

"Ah, Mr. Lincoln," the reporter said. "And why are you in town today?"

"Oh, just by accident," Lincoln answered.

"But, having come, you stayed to hear the Democratic candidate?"

"Yes," Lincoln said. "I always like to hear Judge Douglas. I have known him for years."

"And will you speak in Chicago, sir?"

"I may," said Lincoln. "I may do so."

The next evening, from the same balcony, Lincoln addressed a much smaller gathering. Repeating his "house divided" theme, he said, "Let us discard all this quibbling about this man and that man, this race and that race being inferior to the other. Let us unite as one people, declaring that all men are created equal."

From Chicago, Douglas went to Bloomington, riding in a luxurious private railroad car with Adele, three secretaries, a photographer, correspondents from eastern papers and a coterie of intimate friends. He felt, as Adele did, that he must look his best for his constituency. His suit was of fine blue broadcloth and he had donned a wide-brimmed white hat. At Joliet a flatcar was coupled to the train; on it were two cannon painted with the slogan "Popular Sovereignty," and two youths in military garb, who fired the cannon at each halt. At Bloomington a band awaited Douglas and he was swept into a parade of Democrats, lustily singing "Hail Columbia."

Abraham Lincoln had been the only Republican passenger on the Douglas train. He sat in a rear coach with cinders sifting in upon him. There was no ovation for him at the Bloomington depot. He walked alone to the hotel, a gaunt and faintly comical figure in his ancient black plug hat and loose black alpaca coat, a carpetbag dangling from his arm.

In the hotel washroom a chance acquaintance spied him.

"Well, hello, Abe! Doggin' the Little Giant's tracks, eh?"

Lincoln smiled but said nothing.

Douglas spoke that evening in the Courthouse Square. As he finished, Lincoln got up and announced that he would have liked to add something: "But I do not deem it proper at a meeting called by a Democratic committee. Later in the campaign, I shall speak in Bloomington."

Then he returned to the depot and boarded the Douglas train as it left for Springfield.

Douglas' reception at the state capital was wet but warm. Torrents of rain deluged all the ornate festoons and banners. Nevertheless, the Democrats were out en masse to escort him to their rally in a grove at the edge of the town. Unnoticed, Lincoln strode off toward the grove, taking a short cut, crossing a stubbly meadow, leaping fences as nimbly as a boy, the carpetbag and an unopened umbrella slapping at his knees, his hat askew on his head, the skirts of his coat flying in the wind.

Douglas' Springfield speech delighted his listeners. With pomp and praise they escorted him back to his train. This time Lincoln remained behind and spoke at night in the hall of the statehouse.

The issues of the campaign had been made abundantly clear, Lincoln said. In defending popular sovereignty, Douglas endorsed the repeal of the Missouri Compromise, the Dred Scott Decision, the possible extension of slavery, the "white man's government." Lincoln condemned them all.

"Free men of Sangamon, free men of Illinois, free men everywhere, judge ye between him and me. . . ."

Douglas had set himself an arduous schedule. As he went on with it, his counselors felt that he was doing very well indeed. President Buchanan's enmity seemed not to have harmed him with the voters in his home state; newspapers were changing their tune and conceding that he might be re-elected—and by a sizable margin.

Yes, all omens were auspicious. But the counselors were annoyed by Lincoln's stalking of Douglas. It was ludicrous—and somehow it detracted more from Douglas' dignity than from Lincoln's. How could it be stopped?

Months earlier Horace Greeley, the Republican editor of the *New York Tribune,* had proposed in his columns that the Illinois senatorial candidates canvass the state together and debate the issues jointly. Other leaders in both parties had seconded the proposal. It would be quite in the American tradition, they said. Had not Alexander Hamilton debated with Thomas Jefferson, and Henry Clay with Andrew Jackson, events notable in the country's political history?

Why not Lincoln and Douglas now in 1858?

On July 24, Lincoln wrote to Douglas, inquiring whether he would consent to a canvass of the sort.

Douglas hesitated. He had always been fond of debate; he was experienced, proficient at it. Long ago, as a fledgling politician, he had tried his wings by canvassing his congressional district with John T. Stuart—he remembered, grinning, that he had bitten Stuart's thumb! Since then he had engaged in frequent verbal duels in the House of Representatives, the Senate, nearly always profitably.

But this one would be an inconvenience, a nuisance. Lincoln, a newcomer to the national scene, might gain by the advertising it afforded. Douglas needed no advertising. And why had the challenge been delayed until Douglas' speaking dates were all fixed and he had scarcely an hour to spare? Was it pettifogging, a device by which Lincoln sought to embarrass him?

"And yet I must consent," he said to his counselors. "If I don't the Republican press will scream 'Coward!' The only compensation is that it may keep Old Abe from treading on my heels from now until Election Day—though I can't be positive even of that!"

Concealing his reluctance, he wrote to Lincoln, saying that he wished to "accommodate" him and hoped soon to talk with him about definite details.

Douglas had abandoned his private car and now was traveling from county to county in a phaeton. One afternoon, as he drove from a meeting in Monticello toward Bement where he was to speak at night, he saw a big old-fashioned prairie schooner approaching on the road.

"Look, isn't that Lincoln?" he said to the Democratic committeemen who were in the phaeton. "Yes, it is! Bound for Monticello, to salvage the remnants of my crowd. Pull up, driver." Leaning out, he called to Lincoln: "Good day, sir. Come back to

Bement with us and I'll get you a larger crowd than you'll find at Monticello."

Lincoln jumped down from his cumbersome wagon. "No, thank you, Judge. Of course, I may be in Bement tonight—"

Douglas laughed. "I'm sure you will. By accident! I'd bet on it."

"Maybe we can have our talk—about the joint appearances."

"Yes," said Douglas. "My wife and I will be spending the night with the Bryant family."

Lincoln nodded. "I know the house. I'll find you."

At eleven o'clock that night, Lincoln was ringing the Bryants' doorbell. Everybody had gone to bed, but Mr. Bryant let him in and summoned Douglas, who came downstairs in his nightshirt, dressing gown and slippers. Seated in the lamplit parlor, the candidates talked quietly. By twelve o'clock, when Lincoln trundled away in his prairie schooner, arrangements had been completed for a series of seven debates, an enterprise that would live forever as a colorful American legend.

In the next several weeks Douglas spoke somewhere every day, often twice a day. Adele went with him, never complaining of the hardships of driving through sun and dust, lodging in uncomfortable taverns, eating scanty and unappetizing food, or doing without food if none was available. Republican newspapers, observing her modish costumes, gay spirits and gracious manner, said that Mrs. Douglas was a factor in the campaign— a "dangerous" factor. But was such behavior "ladylike"?

"Mrs. Lincoln," the Republicans pointed out, "is staying at home in Springfield."

The program for the joint canvass did not deter Lincoln from treading on Douglas' heels. He continued to follow the Demo-

cratic entourage as it moved through the state. And once, for a
few hours, he was Adele Douglas' traveling companion. A heavy
rainstorm had made the roads impassable for a horse and carriage. Douglas had hastened on foot to a scheduled meeting,
leaving Adele to come later by train—the same train that bore the
pursuing Mr. Lincoln. Discovering him in the dingy coach,
Adele sat beside him. They chatted cordially, Lincoln seemed
entertained and beguiled.

At the station, where Douglas was waiting for Adele, Lincoln
bade her a smiling good-by.

"Well, Judge," he said, "here's your old 'oman that I brought
along. She probably can do more with you than I can."

Adele had liked Mr. Lincoln very much.

"Why is he pictured as rough and uncouth?" she asked
Douglas. "Mr. Lincoln isn't that at all! He is a true gentleman."

In August Douglas had news that Kansas voters in a supervised election had repudiated the Lecompton constitution. They
preferred to forego statehood for a while rather than adopt a body
of laws tainted with cunning and deceit.

Douglas was greatly elated at this outcome of his relentless
battle with Buchanan and the proslavery plotters. He felt that
he was no longer exiled from his party and—far better—that
popular sovereignty had been exonerated. He said that though
the Dred Scott Decision legalized slavery in Kansas, the Free-
Soilers were numerous enough to restrict and control the system.
He predicted that Kansas would soon be a free state in the
Union.

Now that Lincoln and Douglas were to be seen and heard
together, comparisons of the two candidates were being made.

Journalists friendly to Douglas commented on his courage,
his grasp of national affairs: "Senator Douglas is calm and
deliberate, a practical man with a fine, resonant voice, a dynamic

delivery. He does not lack a sense of humor. He can enjoy a joke, but never has been known to tell one. Instead, he speaks gravely, with logic and conviction."

Lincoln, said these journalists, had none of Douglas' polish and little of his poise. Lincoln was a "rambling" speaker, given to digressing from the subject of discussion. "He is moody, sometimes sober to the verge of melancholy, sometimes displaying flashes of an erratic, even coarse, hilarity. His voice is thin and unmusical, his gestures are awkward."

Perhaps it escaped the notice of Lincoln's critics that he also possessed an instinctive understanding of human nature, a deep sympathy for pain, suffering and deprivation which he was singularly able to express in plain language and, in his thin, unmusical voice, with awkward gestures, to communicate.

# 16

# THE GREAT DEBATES

August 21, 1858, was a typically hot summer day in Lasalle County, Illinois, but the excitement that stirred the town of Ottawa was unprecedented, for this was the time and place of the first debate between the two senatorial aspirants, Lincoln and Douglas.

All morning, farm wagons streamed steadily in from the sun-baked prairies to deposit families of men, women and children in streets that since dawn had churned with bustling townsfolk. Visitors came from nearby villages in buggies, carts, canalboats; a train from Chicago brought seventeen carloads of passengers. By noon dust wafted like a silvery veil over the placards and decorations, the flags, mottoes and flower-furbished floats.

The noise was earsplitting. Peddlers shrilly hawked their wares: *"Douglas buttons! Lincoln badges! A dime apiece, three for a quarter!"* Fife-and-drum corps squealed and rattled, trumpets blared, dogs barked, babies wailed. There were raucous roars for the candidates: *"'Ray for Douglas, the Little Giant!"* *"Go it, Abe! Eat 'im, swaller 'im! Yowee!"* Marshals, each with a dozen deputies, dashed hither and yon, fringed sashes of red, white and blue around their waists, authority in their admonitions: *"Out of the way! No brawling!"*

Today Lincoln had his own special train, fourteen coaches

crammed with shouting Republicans who scrambled down in
the station yard and hurried him into a carriage which the "fair
young ladies of Ottawa" had garlanded with evergreen boughs.
Douglas arrived in a grand barouche with several hundred out-
riders, the men and horses all sporting rosettes and nosegays of
bright ribbon.

At two in the afternoon the marshals ushered the candidates
with their committeemen toward the platform which had been
erected in the square: *"Back! Step back! Make room!"* But thirty
minutes elapsed before Lincoln and Douglas could push through
the throng and mount the platform. Then there was a burst of
frenzied cheering—and, abruptly, a silence.

Side by side they stood, the rivals, and probably an audience
of strangers would have thought them an odd pair: the stocky
Little Giant in city attire of ruffled shirt, silk cravat and well-
tailored blue suit, his eyes very keen and blue in a serenely
smiling countenance; Lincoln tall and angular in misshapen
black garments, his eyes meditative, cheeks furrowed, lips twisted
in a slightly nervous grin. But this audience was familiar with
the looks of Steve Douglas and Old Abe. Let them get on with
their speechifying!

Douglas spoke first: "I shall talk to you for an hour," he said.
"Mr. Lincoln will then have the floor for an hour and a half,
after which I shall have a half-hour for a rejoinder. Mr. Lincoln
and I beg you not to interrupt us with heckling or applause."

With this preliminary over, Douglas mentioned his long acquaintance with Lincoln: "It began when I was a schoolteacher
in Winchester, and he a flourishing grocery keeper in Salem. As
young men we both were elected to the legislature. Mr. Lincoln
was then just as good at telling an anecdote as he is now. He
could beat any of the boys wrestling, or running a footrace, in
pitching quoits or tossing a copper, and the dignity and im-

partiality with which he presided at a horse race or fist fight won the praise of everybody."

There was a ripple of laughter. As it subsided, Douglas went on to outline Lincoln's political career, how he had dropped from the legislature, and from sight, only to emerge somewhat later as a member of Congress—where, it should be remembered, he had voted against the Mexican War, that unprovoked assault of an enemy nation on the United States! He had not been renominated for Congress by his party; forsaken by his former friends he had retired from public life.

"And now Mr. Lincoln has bobbed up again to say that our government cannot be half slave and half free—"

"And he's right!" cried someone in the crowd. "Neither can it!"

"Why not?" asked Douglas. "Washington, Jefferson, Franklin, Madison, our great forefathers made it so. Why cannot it exist on the foundation they gave it?"

"It can, Steve!" cried someone else. "It will!"

Douglas spoke of Abolitionism. Lincoln, he said, was an Abolitionist. Yes, though he might shy from it, he could not elude the label. The Republican party was the party of Abolitionism, and the Republicans of Illinois had chosen Abraham Lincoln to represent them in this contest as their "one and only candidate."

Douglas read the resolutions passed by these Republicans at their June convention, in which they pledged themselves to support every phase of the Abolitionist movement. "As their candidate, Mr. Lincoln cannot do otherwise than to work for the achievement of such goals."

Douglas had some questions he wanted Mr. Lincoln to answer, seven of them. He read the questions; they all pertained to the slavery issue. "Mr. Lincoln's answers will show us either that he is indeed an Abolitionist—or not true to the Republican cause which he has assumed."

Brisk and voluble, Douglas continued until the officials signaled to him that his hour was up. Then, bowing, he took his chair, drew a cigar from his pocket, lighted it and puffed forth clouds of fragrant smoke.

Lincoln rose and came forward to the rostrum's edge. He, too, had something to read. He squinted at a paper in his hand.

"Put on your specs, Abe!" shouted a teasing voice.

"Yes, sir, I'm obliged to. I'm no longer a young man."

The paper was a copy of a speech he had made in 1854. He put on his spectacles and read several paragraphs. In 1854 he had denied that he was an Abolitionist; he denied it now. As for his voting record in Congress: "I was an old Whig, and whenever the Democrats tried to get me to say that the Mexican War had been righteously begun, I wouldn't do it. But whenever they asked for any money, or land warrants, or pay for the soldiers, I gave the same vote that Judge Douglas did."

Reviewing his "house divided" speech, he said that he was unalterably opposed to the extension of slavery, but had no thought of doing anything that might lead to a war between the North and the South, nor could he conceive of such a tragedy. He felt, though, that a conspiracy had been formed to nationalize slavery and that Douglas had entered into it. He spoke of the power exercised by public sentiment: "He who molds public sentiment goes deeper than he who enacts statutes or makes decisions. It must be borne in mind that Judge Douglas is a man of vast influence. Many people profess to believe *anything*, if they find out that Judge Douglas professes to believe it."

Lincoln answered Douglas' questions only vaguely and sat down fifteen minutes before his allotted period had expired.

Douglas sprang up for the rejoinder.

"Smash 'im, Steve! Pour it on!" yelled bellicose Democrats.

Douglas was quite ready to "pour it on."

"Mr. Lincoln will have to prove his charge that I have ever entered into a conspiracy of any sort! On the contrary, I have fought against the nationalization of slavery. Mr. Lincoln will have to deal more satisfactorily with my questions!"

Douglas was still dissecting and analyzing Lincoln's speech when the officials again waved him to a stop.

As if unleashed, the crowd rushed to surround, congratulate and embrace the candidates. Lincoln was seized by two brawny farmers who hoisted him to their shoulders and carried him from the square, his long legs thrust out grotesquely, his trousers pulled up to reveal several inches of his underpants.

"Abe plumb licked the Little Giant!" shrieked the Republicans.

But the Democrats were no less ecstatic. "Abe's done for, he's ruined!" they crowed. "Can't navigate, poor feller! Douglas scared him might' nigh to death!"

The weather was chill and damp for the second debate at Freeport on August 27. In the intervening six days, the candidates had gone their separate paths, speaking in other towns. By coincidence, they were registered at the same hotel in Freeport. At noon they came out, arm in arm, on the veranda and bowed to the populace.

The Republicans had a big Conestoga wagon into which they bundled Lincoln. When Douglas saw the wagon bowling off toward the platform with Lincoln in it, he said that he would walk.

"Lincoln is playing his kinship with the common people to a fare-you-well," he told his committeemen. "His poverty and shabbiness will get him votes by the bushel, and what wealth I've accumulated will be a handicap to me. But I'll not have these people thinking that I'm an aristocrat! So I shall *walk*."

Now the order had been reversed; Lincoln spoke first. Apparently he had studied Douglas' questions, for he answered them tersely, disclaiming any connection with the Abolitionists' radical objectives. And he had four questions to ask Douglas. The most important of them, he said, was whether or not in Douglas' opinion the inhabitants of a territory could by lawful means exclude slavery from the region prior to the adoption of a state constitution. With this question, Lincoln hoped to point out the weaknesses of popular sovereignty.

When it was Douglas' turn, he replied immediately to all of Lincoln's questions, disposing of them neatly. Yes, in his opinion slavery could by lawful means be excluded from a territory prior to the adoption of a state constitution: "And Mr. Lincoln has heard me say so a hundred times from every stump in Illinois!"

He charged Lincoln with shifting his views on slavery as he traveled through Illinois; in the northern counties, he talked like an Abolitionist, in the southern counties, he disparaged Abolitionism.

"But I have never changed and never will," he said. "In 1858, I am just as I was in 1850, 1854 and 1856. Any man who votes for me knows exactly where I stand on every issue."

Lincoln was perhaps startled by Douglas' promptness and candor. In his rejoinder he seemed ill at ease, putting politics aside and telling jokes and amusing stories. The audience, much regaled, laughed and clapped. But the Republican committeemen looked glum. This second debate had been a Douglas victory.

The third meeting, September 15, at Jonesboro attracted a smaller and somewhat apathetic crowd. The day was cool and cloudy. The orators wrangled lengthily about the qualifications of the various candidates for the legislature and read voluminous reports, while the audience fidgeted and yawned.

Jonesboro, in the southernmost part of Illinois, had always been a Democratic stronghold. Lincoln knew that anything he might say here would be doubted. Reverting to the matter of slavery in the territories, he said that Douglas had contradicted himself. If the Dred Scott Decision was valid, people living in a territory could not limit the spread of slavery, for Chief Justice Taney's ruling was the very antithesis of popular sovereignty.

"You might have one," Lincoln said, "but never both."

"Yes, you can," Douglas insisted. "The Kansans will have both."

There was a comet in the sky that night. Douglas had driven on with his committee to his next engagement, but Lincoln, alone and brooding, strolled out from the Jonesboro Hotel to gaze at the comet.

Lincoln's friends regarded the fourth debate, September 18, at Charleston as a "bull's-eye" for their side. The crowd was enormous and enthusiastic. This was Coles County, where old-line Whigs were plentiful. Twenty-eight years earlier, Lincoln with his father, stepmother and a tribe of relatives had passed through Charleston as they migrated to a newly purchased farm in Illinois. Now across the main street the townsfolk had stretched an immense painting of that migration, with Abraham Lincoln depicted as the backwoods youth he then had been. Though the Democrats greeted Douglas with banners, cantering horsemen, firecrackers and resounding huzzas, the Republicans were more numerous and noisier. A splendid brass band had come from Terre Haute, Indiana, to head a procession of elaborate floats on which pretty girls in white robes posed, smiled and pelted the jubilant Republicans with flowers.

At Charleston, and afterward, the speeches were repetitious. The candidates were saying, with few modifications, what they had said from the beginning. The subject was invariably slavery; it was the only real issue—what should or should not be done about it. Douglas made much of the fact that slavery was not prohibited, not even referred to in the Constitution, the hallowed document which would always be his infallible guide. Lincoln countered by saying that the framers of the Constitution had been ashamed of the system, had thought it must surely become extinct and "wanted nothing on the face of the great charter of liberty to suggest that Negro slavery had ever existed among us."

The address of both candidates was sharper now, less courteous, more barbed with sarcasm.

Douglas was bored by Lincoln's harping on the "house divided" theme, bored with his homely stories. He thought Lincoln was evasive, "wishy-washy." He disliked Lincoln's habit of prefacing his statements with equivocal phrases, such as "It may be so," "If I'm not mistaken," or "I guess that was done." Douglas himself was straightforward, hard-hitting, never "guessing," never feeling that he might be mistaken in what he said.

To add to Douglas' irritation, he now was being harassed by a group of Buchanan Democrats whom the President had set upon him, and by roistering Republicans who baited him as he walked or drove down the streets, and serenaded him at night with scurrilous songs and parodies. And he was alarmed, though this he did not confide even to Adele, that his fine voice was tiring, his throat ached from the strain of constant speaking—and that Lincoln seemed unwearied by the grind, Lincoln's voice seemed to improve.

If Lincoln was irked by Douglas, as he sometimes was, it was because of the Little Giant's blindness to the fundamental character of slavery, its underlying evil: "Judge Douglas sees nothing wrong with the system, he cannot distinguish slavery from freedom." Again and again, Lincoln made the charge, saying as often: "But I know slavery to be wrong, morally, socially, politically. I desire a national policy that will prevent its extension and ultimately outlaw it."

Galesburg was another Republican town. Cold rain was falling there on October 7, the wind blew fiercely, but twenty thousand citizens had gathered in the quadrangle of the Knox College campus for the fifth debate, and the windows and roofs of the dormitories were packed with students.

Douglas opened, speaking for an hour in a rather scholarly vein, as befitted, he thought, an audience of educated people, yet knowing that not many of them would ever vote for a Democrat—and dismally fearing that he was too hoarse to be heard beyond the front rows. When Lincoln got up, he renewed his accusation that Douglas had plotted with southern statesmen to nationalize slavery. Douglas was incensed. In the rejoinder period he turned on Lincoln, dared him to produce one single shred of evidence that this was true, and twice shook his fist at him.

But at Quincy where the sixth meeting took place, October 13, Douglas was his normal, calm, good-tempered self. This was his old bailiwick. Here, on the Illinois Supreme Court bench, he had earned an enviable reputation for integrity, from here he had set out for Washington as a young and untried congressman. Hundreds of his friends were at the station to give the Little Giant and his lovely wife a royal welcome.

It was a day of sparkling autumn weather and tremendous commotion, the crowd larger than ever before, the decorations more lavish. Determined not to be overwhelmed by the swarming Democrats, the Republicans rallied, stamped and hooted. Party emblems plastered every fence and wall, bands played incessantly. The Republicans paraded, bearing a pole at the top of which was perched a fat, live raccoon. Behind them frolicked a long line of Democrats with a pole suspending a dead raccoon by its bushy tail.

"Look, we've got Abe!" the Democrats jeered. "Look at all that's left of poor Old Abe!"

Douglas' hoarseness was somewhat relieved and he had recovered the vigor he had seemed to lack at Galesburg. He spoke eloquently and was wildly cheered. But Lincoln's speech was also effective, drawing hearty applause from his partisans.

From Quincy, the candidates rode on the same riverboat down the Mississippi to Alton for the seventh and last debate, October 15. During the joint canvass they had expounded divergent views on governmental policies. At Alton they summarized once more these concepts.

To both, the preservation of the Union, whole and intact, was of utmost importance. Both shrank from the idea of a sectional war. Douglas believed that the catastrophe of war could be avoided only by preserving also the *status quo*, by obedience to the letter of the Constitution and all properly enacted laws, whether federal or local, by sustaining the decisions of duly authorized courts, even when such decisions were stringent and distasteful. Lincoln was for "laying the foundations of new societies," for blocking what he saw as the insidious, purposeful advance of slavery into the territories, for making any effort necessary to eradicate slavery finally and forever.

It would be said by many observers that in the debates Lincoln had fared the better. While their appearances together had probably not hindered Douglas' campaign, they had substantially helped Lincoln's, stimulating interest in his candidacy at home and abroad; as they progressed, Lincoln had seemed to gain the advantage.

"But which man will Illinois send to the Senate?" asked a Chicago editor. "It is a tight race. The result will not be known until Election Day."

Election Day, November 2, was rainy, dreary, raw.

"A day for ducks and Democrats," said the political seers.

And it was. The voting was heavy, Illinois elected a majority of Democratic legislators, who would re-elect Douglas to the Senate when the General Assembly should next convene.

Douglas voted early and then went on to Washington. Springfield Democrats exultantly telegraphed the news to him. The message he wired back was brief: "Let the voice of the people rule."

"And how does it strike *you*, Abe?" queried a disgruntled Republican.

"Well, it hurts too much to laugh," Lincoln said, "and I'm too big to cry!"

# 17

# DARKENING SKIES

In his re-election to the Senate, Douglas had scored an astonishing personal triumph, and at once a hundred Democratic newspapers in the North, from Maine to Missouri, urged his nomination as the party's Presidential candidate in 1860.

But southern Democrats were becoming lukewarm about him. They had liked his popular sovereignty only when it did not impinge upon their hidebound prejudices—and they had never comprehended his frequent avowals that he was neither for nor against slavery. To them, it made no sense: anyone who was not *against* slavery must automatically be *for* it; there was no middle ground. And hadn't he favored the Free-Soilers in Kansas? Beware of wolves in sheep's clothing!

Nor had Buchanan been appeased. Buchanan had wished to see Douglas humiliated in his home state. Foiled and angry, Buchanan and his henchmen worked to curb the rising "Douglas boom."

The campaign in Illinois had wearied Douglas. His doctors diagnosed his throat ailment as serious; they prescribed several weeks of rest. So, early in 1859, with Adele, he made a trip to New Orleans and Cuba. The voyage back on a coastwise ship was pleasant, his throat healed, and soon he told his friends that he was willing to contend for the nomination at the national convention which would be held at Charleston, South Carolina, in the spring of 1860.

"Though the Presidency of the United States is the most exalted office in the world, I am not overly anxious for it," he said. "My feeling is that I shall have more chance of election than any other Democrat. There is a growing bitterness in the South. It is being rumored that if our next President is a Republican, the southern states may try to leave the Union. Secession? We cannot have that! We want peace in the country, a peaceful adjustment of all our problems."

But how difficult to believe in 1859 that peace was possible! Even the dream of peace seemed a bubble blown so thin that the tiniest surface pinprick might deflate it.

This was the year when Senator Jefferson Davis of Mississippi introduced a resolution demanding a slave code for all the territories, when Senator William Seward of New York called the struggle between North and South an "irrepressible conflict." It was the year when there was such tension in Congress that members went to the sessions with guns, daggers and bowie knives under their coats, and armed guards were posted in the galleries with instructions to shoot at the least indication of disturbance on the floor.

It was the year of John Brown's raid.

John Brown was the grim, mysterious visionary who had ambushed and slaughtered five Sons of the South in Kansas at Pottawatomie Creek. Now, in October, 1859, he had come east to Harpers Ferry, Virginia, a little town sixty miles distant from Washington. Aided and abetted by Abolitionist zealots, he attempted to incite a slave insurrection by attacking and capturing the government arsenal at the confluence of the Potomac and Shenandoah rivers.

His plan was fantastic, his band of raiders ridiculously, pitifully small and inept, his seizure and punishment swift. But, hanged on the gallows for the triple crimes of conspiracy, murder and treason, the madman was hailed as a martyr, exploited and immortalized by the Abolitionists in a song that would be a battle cry throughout the four darkest years of American history:

> *John Brown's body lies a-moldering in the grave,*
> *His soul goes marching on. . . .*

In April, 1860, the Democratic national convention was held in Charleston, South Carolina. For a century this most picturesque of American cities had symbolized the fabulous Old South of wealth, fashion and leisure, of inherited aristocracy, chivalry and luxurious hospitality among the magnolias and azaleas—and, less conspicuously, of slave pens and marts where Negroes were bought and sold at auction.

Douglas went to the convention. He had been ill again. He said that he would not fight for the nomination and would accept it only if the party's platform was one that he could execute in all good faith.

The delegates who were for him had no misgivings. "We are in the majority," they said. "The platform will be as you wish it, you cannot lose."

But the meeting in Institute Hall had scarcely opened when the delegates from the slave states began to growl and grumble. They did not intend to be dominated by the northerners. They did not fancy Stephen Douglas, that "little gamecock," and would not cater to his whims. The Democratic party had its taproots in the South; therefore, southerners had a primary claim upon it. Now these Douglas men were making offensive speeches in which they asked for moderation, conservatism, and asserted that slavery was an inflammable subject, to be handled with care.

"Moderation, indeed!" the southerners said. "Slavery is our

bread and butter, our life's blood. It is lawful, it is *right,* and the party must go on record as its protector in any and all of the territories—and everywhere!"

"Never, never!" cried a delegate from Ohio. "Gentlemen of the South, you mistake us. You mistake us! We acknowledge the existence of the slavery, but we cannot, *will not,* say that it is right!"

For a week the convention sparred and quarreled. The southerners, sullen and obdurate, declared that if Douglas' policies were adopted they would get up and leave Institute Hall. And when, on the eighth day, a popular sovereignty platform which Douglas himself had framed was voted through, the Alabama delegation rose in a body and walked out. Then the delegations of Mississippi, Louisiana, Florida, Texas and Arkansas followed suit, to be roundly cheered in the streets of Charleston.

"Hurrah for the South!" shouted onlookers. "Let's have a new southern republic!"

The northern delegates, somewhat crestfallen, sessioned to ballot for a candidate. The first ballot gave Douglas a majority, but not the two-thirds vote that was required for nomination. In several delegations were men who had vowed to avenge Buchanan and would not now budge from their promises. The voting continued, the Buchanan men were relentless. After fifty-seven ballots had been tabulated, and Douglas had never got quite the necessary two-thirds, and everyone's patience was exhausted, the convention adjourned, its members agreeing to meet again (and surely more amicably!) at Baltimore in June.

The Douglas Democrats went away from Charleston fearing that unless the disintegrating strands of their party were rewoven, the next President would be a Republican. It would depend, they said, upon whom the Republicans selected as a standard bearer. Seward of New York seemed the likeliest man.

"I'll withdraw from the race," Douglas told his friends. "I have enemies, both northern and southern. If those enemies would rather destroy the party than have me as its candidate, so be it. My beliefs are adamant. I will not forswear them."

But his friends were many and loyal; and at the Baltimore convention, June 18, he was nominated on the second ballot as the Democratic candidate.

Meanwhile, the Charleston bolters were organizing. On June 28, they chose as their candidate John C. Breckinridge of Kentucky, the Vice-President of the United States in Buchanan's administration and a proslavery advocate. And there were other contenders, too. A smaller faction of Democratic dissenters had coalesced as the Constitutional Union party and put John Bell of Tennessee into the field.

And at Chicago, May 16, in a huge garish wooden structure which they called their Wigwam, the Republicans had named, not Seward or any prominent statesman, but Abraham Lincoln of Illinois.

The Douglas men were encouraged by Lincoln's nomination.

"Neither Breckinridge nor Bell has the ghost of a chance," they said. "Lincoln is your only real opponent—and he's a nonentity. You've beaten Lincoln once. You can beat him again."

Douglas nodded quietly. But to Republican acquaintances in Washington, he said: "Gentlemen, you have nominated a very able and a very honest man."

Did he foresee the course of coming events? Had he some uncanny premonition of the near future, his own and his country's?

Later it would be remarked that after the Baltimore convention,

Douglas seemed curiously preoccupied. He prepared to wage a strenuous campaign; it was his obligation, for the party's sake, to do so, and he had never shirked an obligation. But his manner suggested that he felt this would be his last contest with an old rival, that this time the cards were stacked against him—that whether or not he won in November did not weigh so much with him as something else, something valued more dearly.

Companioned by Adele, he went into New England, to Cambridge, where he spoke at Harvard University. In the summer of 1858, he had written a letter to Harvard's president, Dr. Walker, recommending Robert Lincoln, "the young son of my friend, Abraham Lincoln" as a student. Dr. Walker had read the letter to his faculty.

"Abraham Lincoln? Has anyone heard of him?"

No one had, except Professor James Russell Lowell.

"Yes," said Lowell. "Lincoln is that Illinois lawyer who is debating with Senator Douglas."

Because of the senator's letter, the lawyer's son had been admitted to Harvard.

From Cambridge, the Douglases went to New York, stopping in Canandaigua for a visit with the Grangers. That was a joyful day with Sarah hostess at a picnic-style dinner for fifty people.

"Oh, Stephen!" she said, in a flutter of pride and excitement. "Look! The yard is jammed with folks waiting to shake hands with you. And all these banners and the grand music. Stephen, you're the biggest frog in the puddle. The biggest and the *best!*"

He went to Vermont, to Brandon, and placed a wreath of flowers on his father's grave and spoke to the villagers.

"I won't get many votes in rock-ribbed New England," he told Adele. "But I'm retracing the steps of my childhood, refreshing my memories of that far-off time."

He traveled through New Hampshire, Maine, Rhode Island,

then into Virginia. In Norfolk people were boldly talking of secession. At a public meeting he was given a slip of paper on which two questions were penciled.

"Answer the questions, Senator! Answer, if you can!"

"I can. I will." He read the first question: " 'If Abraham Lincoln be elected President, will the southern states be justified in seceding from the Union?' " He flung back his mane of gray-streaked hair and thundered, "I emphatically answer *No!*" He read the second question; " 'If they secede upon the inauguration of Abraham Lincoln, will you advise or uphold resistance?' My answer is *No!* I will do all in my power to aid in maintaining the laws of the nation against all resistance to them, *from whatever quarter it might come!*"

There was the merest patter of applause. His answers did not please the citizens of Norfolk.

At Raleigh he spoke of his devotion to the Union. "I love the Union. I love my children, but I do not desire to see them survive this Union!"

The audience murmured and scowled. There was no applause at all.

On and on he journeyed—into Ohio, Indiana, Iowa. His throat troubled him, his voice was rough and husky, but he spoke earnestly, with an absolute dedication: "It is not ambition that impels me to this campaign. The Presidency has no charms for me. But our country is in peril. The Union must be preserved and I would make any sacrifice on earth to preserve it."

Wisconsin, Michigan, Missouri. . . . He told his secretary, "Mr. Lincoln will be the next President. It is inevitable. I know the signs."

"And that will be a tragedy," said the secretary.

"Not for me," Douglas said. "The tragedy will be America's —if the South secedes. I'm going South again."

Tennessee, Alabama, Georgia. . . . For weeks he spoke twice or three times a day, from hotel verandas, from the rear of railroad coaches, in barns, churches, wherever he could get a hearing.

"You have wonderful stamina, Senator Douglas," said a journalist, "a marvelous constitution. Is it the Constitution of the United States?"

The pun amused him and, tired as he was, he laughed. "Yes, sir. Yes, that's just what I have."

But his wonderful stamina was being gruelingly tested. Adele was worried. "You're worn out, Stephen. Haggard!"

"I have a job to do," he said. "Maybe I can't bring it off, maybe no one could save the Union. Still, I must *try.*"

The southern tour was fraught with distressing incidents. Once the cotton states had admired Stephen Douglas as the most steadfast exponent of states' rights. Now he was setting the rights of the Union above those of the individual states, saying that, whatever the provocation, the South must not, *could* not, secede.

"Secession is illegal, criminal! Banish it from your thoughts!"

This was gross insolence, which must be treated with insolence. Newspapers insulted him; crowds hissed and sneered at him. Rocks, tomatoes, eggs were thrown at him; vandals endeavored to wreck the trains on which he rode.

Undeterred, he plodded on, begging for tolerance, peace: "My fellow Americans, the Union cannot be dissolved!"

He was in Mobile on Election Day. He spent the evening in the editorial rooms of the *Mobile Register,* scanning dispatches from the North as they filtered in. Before midnight it was apparent that Lincoln had won.

The editor of the *Register* said that his paper would promote a state convention to define Alabama's role in the secession movement.

"No, no!" Douglas protested. "In a convention of that kind, the friends of the Union would be outvoted—"

"But the people of Alabama are not friends of the Union, Senator Douglas. As you well know, the Union has few friends anywhere in the South. The slave states have said that if a Republican President were elected, they would secede. That was not an empty boast. It is their fixed intention."

"But perhaps something can be done, an eleventh-hour compromise—"

"I think not," said the editor. "Tonight the corner has been turned."

Infinitely sad, his broad shoulders sagging, Douglas walked slowly back through darkened streets to his hotel.

# 18

# TIME OF CRISIS

Douglas clung tenaciously, desperately, to his hope for an eleventh-hour easing of the national crisis, but the days and weeks went by, rapidly and inexorably, and no such miracle occurred.

In December, 1860, South Carolina seceded from the Union. In January and February of 1861, Mississippi and Florida, Alabama and Georgia, Louisiana and Texas seceded. The seven states would soon be joined by Virginia, Arkansas, Tennessee and North Carolina to form the Confederate States of America, with Jefferson Davis as provisional President. The Confederacy girded for war and, by mid-February, had taken over southern forts and arsenals, and was mustering and drilling armed troops.

In Washington all was suspense and confusion. Government officials of southern birth or sympathy were resigning from their various departments, army and navy officers resigning their commissions to enlist in southern service. Many civilians, too, were closing their houses and quitting the city.

Mr. Buchanan, after much wavering, had cast his lot with the North. A detachment of United States soldiers commanded by Major Robert Anderson was marooned in Fort Sumter in Charleston Harbor, with a very meager supply of food and ammunition, and confronted by the muzzles of Confederate cannon. Major Anderson sent word of his predicament to Buchanan, who then ordered one ship, *Star of the West,* to sail to Fort Sumter. But when, repulsed by fire from the South Carolina shore batteries, the ship dropped back into northern waters, Buchanan did nothing more to relieve Major Anderson. Bewildered and vacillating, Buchanan marked time. He was unequal to the emergency, he would wait and let the new President cope with it.

On February 11, Lincoln bade his Springfield neighbors goodby and with his family started eastward for his inauguration. He knew that southerners hated him; he had been told that he might be mobbed as his train passed through Baltimore. At the insistence of his bodyguards, he put on a felt hat, pulled down to shield his face, and a large enveloping shawl and, thus disguised, proceeded from Baltimore to Washington, unheralded and unrecognized.

Southerners, and those northerners who had little confidence in him, were quick to say that he was frightened: "Lincoln is a weakling! He *creeps* to the Presidency. Why can't he enter Washington like a *man?*"

But there were friends, Douglas among them, to defend him.

"Lincoln is not weak," said Douglas, "nor is he frightened. He is every inch a man, and one to be trusted!"

Adele Douglas hastened to call upon Mrs. Lincoln, a gracious little courtesy that Mary Lincoln appreciated. Rather dazed by her abrupt transition from Illinois housewife to First Lady of the Land, Mrs. Lincoln welcomed the friendship of a woman of Mrs. Stephen Douglas' wide social experience.

When Lincoln had been three days in Washington, Douglas went to see him. For hours, they talked and conferred.

As Douglas was leaving, he said: "You and I have been for many years politically opposed, sir. But in our fidelity to the Constitution and the Union we have never differed and never will. In this we are as one."

Tears glinted in Lincoln's eyes. "God bless you, Douglas. I thank you with all my heart," he said. "With God to help us, all may yet be well."

Newspapers printed the story of Douglas' conference with Lincoln, and of subsequent conferences, for now they were often closeted together.

"And will you attend the inauguration of the man who defeated you, Senator?" asked a reporter.

"Yes, I shall be there," said Douglas. "And if any person attacks Mr. Lincoln, he attacks me also."

March 4, 1861, dawned cloudy but mild; by noon the weather was bright and summery. A military escort fetched Lincoln from his suite in the Willard Hotel. Seated in the Presidential carriage was James Buchanan, dapper and white-haired, smiling, delighted to be shunting off responsibilities of which he had never been capable. As Lincoln got into the carriage, he exchanged courteous greetings with Buchanan. Lincoln's black coat was new and fine, his stovepipe hat black and shiny, and he had in his hand a huge gold-knobbed cane that had been presented to him for this historic occasion.

Behind the carriage rolled a long procession of vehicles, spaced with military bands and squads of marching infantrymen. To the sound of brisk music the procession wound smartly toward the Capitol. Flags billowed, cannon volleyed salutes; but the crowd in the street was oddly quiet. Riflemen were to be glimpsed on the roofs of houses and a battery of artillery frowned from the brow of Capitol Hill.

The procession halted at the east side of the Capitol, where a balcony had been built. Lincoln and Buchanan came out upon the balcony, followed by the Supreme Court Justices, somber as crows in their flowing black robes. Gradually the balcony filled with members of the Diplomatic Corps and of the Congress. Below were the people, a hushed, expectant mass.

Lincoln was introduced by Senator Baker of Oregon. He bowed and fumbled with his hat, his gold-knobbed cane. Douglas, seated in a chair near the lectern, instantly realized Lincoln's embarrassment with the unwieldy things. Smiling, Douglas leaned forward and lifted the hat and cane out of the way and held them on his knee.

Lincoln had the manuscript of his speech in his coat pocket. He extracted it, settled his glasses on his nose and read the speech, his voice throbbing with feeling.

He would not interfere, he said, with the domestic institutions of the South, or with any of the safeguards of the Constitution, but he believed in the Union. By his reasoning, a state could not possibly secede from the Union, which had been created to endure forever. Any such desertion must be viewed as insurrection or, if on a large scale, as revolution. His purpose would be to see that all the laws of the Union were executed in all the states.

". . . We are not enemies, but friends. We must not be enemies. Though passion may have strained, it must not break our bonds of affection. The mystic chords of memory . . . will yet swell the chorus of the Union, when again touched, as surely they will be, by the better angels of our nature."

Lincoln was visibly moved, but his palm lay flat and firm on the Bible as Chief Justice Roger Taney administered the oath of office.

Then, turning, he retrieved his hat and cane from Douglas.

"Mr. President, I congratulate you," Douglas said. "I am with you now and to the end."

Lincoln's austere countenance softened into a smile of gratitude.

That evening at the Inaugural Ball, Senator Douglas had the honor of leading in the new President's wife. Mary Lincoln's gown was blue, she had thrust a feather ornament into her coiled brown hair. Perhaps, as she danced with Stephen Douglas, she thought of other balls, long ago, when the Little Giant had been her partner. . . .

"Miss Todd, may I have this waltz?"

"Oh yes, Mr. Douglas."

On April 6, Lincoln notified South Carolina that an expedition was en route to Charleston Harbor with provisions for Major Anderson and his beleaguered garrison in Fort Sumter. The Confederacy responded by demanding that the fort be immediately surrendered. When Major Anderson would not surrender, the southern guns opened fire on the fort. For thirty-four hours Anderson withstood a savage bombardment; finally on April 13, at two-thirty in the afternoon, he was forced to haul down the Stars and Stripes from his crumbling ramparts.

Tumult reigned in Washington. Fort Sumter had fallen! This was war!

At dusk of that day, Mr. George Ashmun, a Republican congressman, sped to the home of Senator Douglas.

"The President sent me," Mr. Ashmun said. "You must come to the White House at once."

Douglas hesitated. "It might be considered presumptuous, an intrusion—"

"No, no! He needs you."

"Go, Stephen," said Adele. "Go with Mr. Ashmun."

At the White House, Lincoln received Douglas with outstretched hands. Lincoln had drafted a proclamation to be published the next morning; he asked Douglas to examine it.

"I see you're calling for seventy thousand volunteers," Douglas said, glancing up from the proclamation. "I should have made it two hundred thousand, Mr. President. I know you could get them."

Lincoln had on his desk a map of the government's fortifications. He asked Douglas to look at the map, nodded as Douglas pointed out spots that might be strengthened.

"General Winfield Scott is the ranking officer in the United States Army," Lincoln said. "Will you give your ideas about reinforcements to Scott?"

"Certainly, and the General will know whether they are of merit. I do not pretend to be a military expert," said Douglas.

This time as Douglas was leaving the White House, Mr. Ashmun detained him. "May I have a word with you, Senator?"

"Yes, Mr. Ashmun."

"The President's proclamation will be telegraphed to every northern town and village tonight," Ashmun said. "It is, of course, a declaration of war. A report of your consultation with Mr. Lincoln should go out with it. The war will jolt our people. Even though they've seen its sinister approach, they are not ready for it. Perhaps they think of it as a Republican war, a war of politicians. They will be reassured to know that you are advising with the President. I'll write the report, if you wish, and you can sign—though it would be more effective if *you* wrote it."

"Very well," Douglas said. "Let us stop at your rooms at the Willard Hotel and I'll write it. I shall tell the people that this is a war of all our citizens, that party affiliations mean nothing now."

"Thank you," Ashmun said. "There's no estimating the good you may accomplish by that, Senator, for you are the most eminent man in the North, the most respected, and much better known than the President himself."

Hardly had the proclamation and Douglas' message flashed over the wires than he was besieged with inquiries. He answered sturdily, repeatedly, that he had written in all sincerity: "I am for my country against all assailants. I deprecate war, but if it must come, we can have but two parties—the party of patriots and the party of traitors. All good Democrats belong to the party of patriots."

The firing on Fort Sumter brought forth a tremendous surge of patriotic fervor in the North. Lincoln's call for volunteers was oversubscribed, regiments were quickly recruited. But Douglas learned that Illinois was lagging with its quota of soldiers.

"I'm going to Springfield," he said to Adele. "There is some proslavery feeling in the southern counties of the state. Yes, there always has been—and now we can't tolerate it. The legislature is in session. I must speak to the legislators."

He went by train and at Bellaire, Ohio, just south of Wheeling, Virginia, he was delayed by a faulty connection—a mishap that was to have consequences.

Slavery had never flourished in the northwestern area of Virginia. The people were not secessionists in spirit, their industries were coal mining and manufacturing. They had lamented Virginia's withdrawal from the Union and were not inclined to fight for the Confederacy. When they heard that Senator Douglas was in Bellaire, thousands of them crossed the Ohio River to ask him what they might do in this dilemma.

"The thing to do is to turn from rebellion," he told them. "Unite as brothers. Be true to your government, its President and its colors."

They listened soberly and believed him. Within thirty days, the Unionists of the area were taking steps that would separate them from Virginia and lead them, in 1863, to statehood as West Virginia.

Douglas spoke at Columbus and at Indianapolis. Reaching Springfield at last, he rushed into the statehouse, surprising the legislators by springing to the rostrum.

"Illinois cannot falter in its loyalty," he shouted. "You know me. You know that I have worked and prayed for peace, for a reconciliation between the North and the South. But peace is a vanished dream. Our beloved country is at war. I believe truly, conscientiously, that it is our duty, a duty to ourselves, our children and to God, to support President Lincoln and the Stars and Stripes."

He did not speak in vain. The legislators stamped and applauded. One legislator beckoned him aside. "Douglas," he said, "if you hadn't come, we might have had a little civil war of our own here in Illinois. You have done what nobody else could do. You've put fifty thousand men into Lincoln's service from this state alone."

As it happened, Ulysses S. Grant was in Springfield that very day and Douglas talked with him. Grant had been a captain in the United States Army, but had retired and was now living in Galena.

Grant was to say in later years: "When the war broke out, I decided to go back into the army. I had been offered a Confederate commission, but after hearing Douglas I decided to seek a commission as a mustering officer with the Illinois troops. I owe Stephen A. Douglas an immeasurable debt of gratitude. My entire career I owe to that decision, and to him."

On May 1, Douglas was in Chicago. How strange and varied had been his homecomings during the years! And this one exceeded in strangeness any that had preceded it, for he was met by a vast throng that was nonpolitical, composed of Democrats and Republicans alike, a throng that received him with unbridled enthusiasm and swept him from the station, through the streets to the Wigwam and lifted him to the stage.

"Speak, Douglas! Speak to us!"

He spoke simply, dramatically, tearfully, and said in closing: "There are only two sides to the present issue. We must be for our country or against it. *I am for it!*"

And then it was the last week of May, and he was very ill.

"Physical exhaustion," the Chicago doctors said, "complicated by rheumatism and a raging fever."

Adele was with him. Anxious and fearful, she sent for his Washington doctor, who was a throat specialist. She sent for his mother and Sarah, and for his sons Robert and Stephen Junior who were away at boarding school.

Delirious, racked with agonizing pain, he muttered incoherently, "Telegraph to the President—let the column march on—"

Early in the morning of June 3, he looked up at Adele as she bent over his bed and asked her to open the windows, throw back the curtains.

"Where are my boys?"

"They're coming, Stephen. They'll soon be here." She knelt, slipped her arm under his shoulders and raised him gently from the pillow. "Is there something you want me to tell the boys?"

"Yes," he said, and suddenly his voice and mind were quite clear, he was himself again. "Yes. *Tell them to obey the laws and support the Constitution of the United States!*"

## STEPHEN ARNOLD DOUGLAS IS DEAD

The newspaper bulletin, printed in enormous black letters, rocked America. Throughout the North public buildings were draped with black crepe. The flags of every northern regiment were at half-mast. Millions of people, rich and poor, famous and obscure, were grief-stricken.

In Washington, in an upper room of the White House, Abraham Lincoln stood at a window, staring out at the black streamers that hung from the portico, weeping for the man who had been his rival and his friend.

"Douglas is gone," Lincoln had said to his staff. "This is a cruel sorrow. I must bear it in solitude."

The funeral in Chicago on June 7 was the occasion for the largest demonstration of mourning the city had ever seen, as the Little Giant was borne to his grave on the shore of Lake Michigan. If, in life, Stephen Douglas had made enemies, they were silent now. What remained was the memory of a great and resourceful political leader, a man of courage, generous in defeat, faithful to his convictions and obligations, with an extraordinary capacity for warm human relations and an unswerving love for his native land.

# APPENDICES

In the first debate of the rival candidates at Ottawa, August 21, 1858, Douglas demanded Lincoln's reply to seven specific interrogations. At Freeport, August 27, Lincoln posed four such questions for Douglas to answer. These interrogations and the answers to them assumed importance in the senatorial campaign and were frequently referred to by both men during the course of the debates.

The questions and answers were:

DOUGLAS: I desire to know whether Lincoln today stands as he did in 1854, in favor of the unconditional repeal of the fugitive slave law.

LINCOLN: I do not now, nor ever did, stand in favor of the unconditional repeal of the fugitive slave law.

DOUGLAS: I desire him to answer whether he stands pledged today, as he did in 1854, against the admission of any more slave states into the Union.

LINCOLN: I do not now, nor ever did, stand pledged against the admission of any more slave states into the Union. . . . I would be exceedingly sorry ever to be put in a position of having to pass upon that question. I should be exceedingly glad to know that there would never be another slave state admitted into the Union; but I must add, that if slavery shall be kept out of the territories during the territorial existence of any one given territory, and then the people shall, having a fair chance and a clear field, when they come to adopt the Constitution, do such an extraordinary thing as to adopt a slave constitution, uninfluenced by the actual presence of the institution among them, I see no alternative, if we own the country, but to admit them into the Union.

DOUGLAS: I want to know whether he stands pledged against the admission of a new state into the Union with such a constitution as the people of that state may see fit to make.

LINCOLN: I do not stand pledged against the admission of a new state into the Union with such a constitution as the people of that state may see fit to make.

DOUGLAS: I want to know whether he stands pledged to the abolition of slavery in the District of Columbia.

LINCOLN: I do not stand today pledged to the abolition of slavery in the District of Columbia. . . . I should be exceedingly glad to see slavery abolished in the District of Columbia. I believe that Congress possesses the constitutional power to abolish it. Yet as a member of Congress, I should not with my present views be in favor of endeavoring to abolish slavery in the District of Columbia unless it would be upon these conditions: that the abolition should be gradual, that it should be on a vote of the majority of qualified voters in the District, and that compensation should be made to unwilling owners.

DOUGLAS: I desire him to answer whether he stands pledged to the prohibition of the slave trade between the different states.

LINCOLN: I do not stand pledged to the prohibition of the slave trade between the different states. . . . I am pledged to do nothing about it. It is a subject to which I have not given that mature consideration that would make me feel authorized to state a position so as to hold myself entirely bound by it.

DOUGLAS: I desire to know whether he stands pledged to

prohibit slavery in all the territories of the United States, north as well as south of the Missouri Compromise line.

LINCOLN: I am impliedly, if not expressly, pledged to a belief in the right and duty of Congress to prohibit slavery in all the United States territories.

DOUGLAS: I desire him to answer whether he is opposed to the acquisition of any new territory unless slavery is prohibited therein.

LINCOLN: I am not generally opposed to honest acquisition of territory; and, in any given case, I would or would not oppose such acquisition, accordingly as I might think such acquisition would or would not aggravate the slavery question among ourselves.

LINCOLN: If the people of Kansas shall, by means entirely unobjectionable in all other respects, adopt a state constitution, and ask admission into the Union under it, before they have the requisite number of inhabitants—some ninety-three thousand—will you vote to admit them?

DOUGLAS: I answer . . . that, it having been decided that Kansas has people enough for a slave state, I hold that she has enough for a free state.

LINCOLN: Can the people of a United States territory, in any lawful way, against the wish of any citizen of the United States, exclude slavery from its limits prior to the formation of a state constitution?

DOUGLAS: I answer emphatically, as Mr. Lincoln has heard me answer a hundred times from every stump in Illinois, that in my opinion the people of a territory can, by lawful means, exclude slavery from their limits prior to the formation of a state constitution. . . . He heard me argue the Nebraska bill on that principle all over the state in 1854, in 1855 and in 1856. . . . It matters not what way the Supreme Court may hereafter decide as to the abstract question whether slavery may or may not go into a territory under the Constitution, the people have the lawful means to introduce it or to exclude it as they please, for the reason that slavery cannot exist a day or an hour anywhere unless it is supported by the local police regulations. Those police regulations can only be established by the local legislature, and if the people are opposed to slavery they will elect representatives to that body who will by unfriendly legislation effectually prevent the introduction of it into their midst. If, on the contrary, they are for it, their legislation will favor its extension.

LINCOLN: If the Supreme Court of the United States shall decide that states cannot exclude slavery from their limits, are you in favor of acquiescing in, adopting and following such decision as a rule of political action?

DOUGLAS: Mr. Lincoln's object is to cast an imputation upon the Supreme Court. . . . It is true that an article published on the 17th of last December put forth that doctrine, and I denounced the article on the floor of the Senate . . . and I was the first man who did. Mr. Lincoln casts an imputation upon the Supreme Court by supposing that they would violate the Constitution of the United States. I tell him that such a thing is not possible. It would be an act of moral treason that no man on the bench could ever descend to.

LINCOLN: Are you in favor of acquiring additional territory, in disregard of how such acquisition may affect the nation on the slavery question?

DOUGLAS: I answer that whenever it becomes necessary in our growth and progress to acquire more territory, I am in favor of it, without reference to the question of slavery, and when we have acquired it, I will leave the people free to do as they please, either to make it slave or free territory, as they prefer.

## EXCERPTS FROM THE LINCOLN-DOUGLAS DEBATES

At Ottawa, La Salle County, August 21, 1858.

DOUGLAS: I do not hold that because the Negro is our inferior therefore he ought to be a slave. On the contrary, I hold that humanity and Christianity both require that the Negro shall have and enjoy every right, every privilege and every immunity consistent with the safety of the society in which he lives. . . . The question then arises, what rights and privileges are consistent with the common good? This is a question which each state and each territory must decide for itself—Illinois has decided it for herself. We have provided that the Negro shall not be a slave, and we have also provided that he shall not be a citizen, but protect him in his civil rights, in his life, his person and his property, only depriving him of all political rights whatsoever, and refusing to put him on an equality with the white man. That policy of Illinois is satisfactory to the Democratic party and to me.

. . . I hold that Illinois had a right to abolish and prohibit slavery as she did, and that Kentucky has the same right to continue and protect slavery that Illinois had to abolish it. I hold that New York has as much right to abolish slavery as Virginia has to continue it, and that each and every state of this Union is a sovereign power, with the right to do as it pleases upon this question of slavery and upon all its domestic institutions.

. . . This doctrine of Mr. Lincoln, of uniformity among the institutions of the different states, is a new doctrine, never dreamed of by Washington, Madison, or the framers of this government. Mr. Lincoln and the Republican party set themselves up as wiser than these men who made this government, which has flourished for seventy years under the principle of popular sovereignty. . . . I believe that this new doctrine preached by Mr. Lincoln and his party will dissolve the Union if it succeeds. They are trying to array all the northern states in one body against the South, to excite a sectional war between the free states and the slave states, in order that the one or the other may be driven to the wall. . . .

LINCOLN: I have no purpose to introduce political and social equality between the white and the black races. There is a physical difference between the two which, in my judgment, will probably forever forbid their living together upon the footing of perfect equality; and inasmuch as it becomes a necessity that there must be a difference, I, as well as Judge Douglas, am in favor of the race to which I belong having the superior position. I have never said anything to the contrary, but I hold that, notwithstanding all this, there is no reason in the world why the Negro is not entitled to all the natural rights enumerated in the Declaration of Independence—the right to life, liberty and the pursuit of happiness. . . .


At Jonesboro, Union County, September 15, 1858.

DOUGLAS: . . . I hold that a Negro is not and never ought to be a citizen of the United States. . . . In my opinion the signers of the Declaration [of Independence] had no reference to the Negro whatever, when they declared all men to be created equal. They desired to express by that phrase white men, men of European birth and European descent. . . . One great evidence that such was their understanding is to be found in the fact that at that time every one of the thirteen colonies was a slaveholding colony, every signer of the Declaration represented a slaveholding constituency, and we know that no one of them emancipated his slaves, much less offered citizenship to them, when they signed the Declaration.

. . . I am in favor of preserving this government as our fathers made it. . . . If we live up to the principle of state rights and state sovereignty, each state regulating its own affairs and minding its own business, we can go on and extend indefinitely just as fast and as far as we need the territory. . . . I never have inquired, and never will inquire, whether a new state applying for admission has slavery or not. . . . If the constitution that is presented be the act and deed of the people, and embodies their will, and they have the requisite population, I will admit them with slavery or without it, just as that people shall determine.

. . . The great mission of the Democracy is to unite the fraternal feeling of the whole country, restore peace and quiet, and all to unite in carrying out the Constitution as our fathers made it, and thus to preserve the Union and render it perpetual in all time to come.

LINCOLN: I say when this government was first established, it was the policy of its founders to prohibit the spread of slavery into the new territories of the United States, where it had not existed. . . . Judge Douglas and his friends have placed it upon a new basis by which it is to become national and perpetual. All I have asked or desired anywhere is that it should be placed back again upon the basis that the fathers of our government originally placed it. I have no doubt that it would become extinct, for all time to come, if we but readopted the policy of the fathers by restricting it . . . from the new territories.

. . . Have we not always had quarrels and difficulties over slavery? And when will we cease to have quarrels over it? Like causes produce like effects. It is worthwhile to observe that we have generally had comparative peace upon the slavery question, and that there has been no cause for alarm until it was excited by the effort to spread it into new territory. . . . It was thus at the date of the Missouri Compromise. It was so again with the annexation of Texas; so with the territory acquired by the Mexican War; and it is so now. Whenever there has been an effort to spread it there has been agitation and resistance. . . . Do you think that the nature of man will be changed—that the same causes that produced agitation at one time will not have the same effect at another? . . .

At Charleston, Coles County, September 18, 1858.

LINCOLN: I do not mean that when it [slavery] takes a turn toward ultimate extinction it will be in a day, nor in a year, nor in two years. I do not suppose that in the most peaceful way ultimate extinction would occur in less than a hundred years at least; but that it will occur in the best way for both races, in God's own time, I have no doubt.

At Galesburg, Knox County, October 7, 1858.

DOUGLAS: . . . Why this attempt, then, to bring the Supreme Court into disrepute among the people? It looks as if there was an effort being made to destroy public confidence in the highest judicial tribunal on earth. Suppose he [Lincoln] succeeds in destroying public confidence in the court, so that the people will not respect its decisions and will feel at liberty to disregard them, and resist the laws of the land, what will he have gained? He will have changed the government from one of laws into that of a mob, in which the strong arm of violence will be substituted for the decisions of the courts of justice.

LINCOLN: The judge [Douglas] has alluded to the Declaration of Independence, and insisted that Negroes are not included in that Declaration . . . and he asks you: Is it possible to believe that Mr. Jefferson, who penned the immortal paper, could have supposed himself applying the language of that instrument to the Negro race, and yet held a portion of that race in slavery? . . . I believe the entire records of the world, from the date of the Declaration up to within three years ago, may be searched in vain for one single affirmation, from one single man, that the Negro was not included in the Declaration of Independence. . . . And I will remind Judge Douglas that while Mr. Jefferson was the owner of slaves, in speaking upon this very subject, he used the strong language that "he trembled for his country when he remembered that God was just." . . . Now I confess myself as belonging to that class in the country who contemplate slavery as a moral, social and political evil . . . who desire a policy that looks to the prevention of it as a wrong, and looks hopefully to the time when as a wrong it may come to an end.


At Quincy, Adams County, October 13, 1858.

LINCOLN: The Republican party think it [slavery] a wrong . . . a wrong not confining itself merely to the persons or the states where it exists, but a wrong which in its tendency affects the existence of the whole nation. . . . We propose a course of policy that shall deal with it as a wrong . . . in so far as we can prevent its growing any larger and that in the run of time there may be some promise of an end to it. . . . He [Douglas] has the high distinction, so far as I know, of never having said slavery is either right or wrong. Almost everybody else says one or the other, but Judge Douglas never does. . . .

. . . You [certain Illinois Democrats] say it is wrong; but don't you constantly object to anybody else saying so? Do you not constantly argue that this is not the right place to oppose it? You say it must not be opposed in the free states, because slavery is not there; it must not be opposed in the slave states, because it is there; it must not be opposed in politics, because that will make a fuss; it must not be opposed in the pulpit, because it is not religion. Then where is the place to oppose it? There is no place to oppose it. There is no plan in the country to oppose this evil overspreading the continent. . . .

DOUGLAS: He [Lincoln] tells you that I will not argue the question whether slavery is right or wrong. I tell you why I will not do it. I hold that, under the Constitution, each state of this Union has a right to do as it pleases on the subject of slavery. . . . I take the decisions of the Supreme Court as the law of the land, and I intend to obey them as such.

I hold that the people of the slaveholding states are civilized men as well as ourselves; that they bear consciences as well as we, and that they are accountable to God and their posterity, and not to us. It is for them to decide, therefore, the moral and religious right of the slavery question for themselves within their own limits. I assert that they had as much right under the Constitution to adopt the system of policy which they have as we had to adopt ours. So it is with every other state in this Union. . . . If we will stand by that principle [state's rights] Mr. Lincoln will find that this republic can exist forever divided into free and slave states. . . . Stand by that great principle, and we can go on as we have done, increasing in wealth, in population, in power, and in all the elements of greatness, until we shall be the admiration and terror of the world.

At Alton, Madison County, October 15, 1858.

DOUGLAS: When the time arrives that I cannot proclaim my political creed in the same terms not only in the northern but the southern states, and wherever the American flag flies over American soil, then there must be something wrong in that creed. Any political creed is radically wrong which cannot be proclaimed in every state and every section of the Union, alike. . . . This government was made upon the great basis of the sovereignty of the states, the right of each state to regulate its own domestic institutions. . . . Our fathers knew that in a republic as broad as this, having such a variety of soil, climate and interest, there must necessarily be a corresponding variety of local laws—the policy and institutions of each state adapted to its conditions and wants. . . . Are you now prepared to abandon the principle and declare that merely because we have the power you will wage a war against the southern states and their institutions until you force them to abolish slavery forever?

The only remedy and safety is that we shall stand by the Constitution . . . obey the laws as they are passed . . . and sustain the decision of the Supreme Court and the constituted authorities.

LINCOLN: The real issue—that will continue in this country when these poor tongues of Judge Douglas and myself shall be silent—is the eternal struggle between right and wrong throughout the world. It is the same in whatever shape it develops itself. . . . Whenever the issue can be distinctly made, and all extraneous matter thrown out, so that men can fairly see the real difference between the parties, this controversy will soon be settled, and it will be done peaceably too. There will be no war, no violence. . . .

# BIBLIOGRAPHY

Beveridge, Albert J.: *Abraham Lincoln.* Boston and New York, Houghton Mifflin Company, 1928.

Brown, William Garrott: *Stephen Arnold Douglas.* Boston and New York, Houghton Mifflin Company, 1902.

Carr, Clark E.: *Stephen A. Douglas, His Life, Public Services, Speeches and Patriotism.* Chicago, A. C. McClurg and Company, 1909.

Flint, Henry Martin: *Life of Stephen A. Douglas, United States Senator from Illinois.* New York, H. Dayton, Publisher, 1860.

Howland, Louis: *Stephen A. Douglas.* New York, Charles Scribner's Sons, 1920.

Johnson, Allen: *Stephen A. Douglas, A Study in American Politics.* New York, The Macmillan Company, 1908.

Lincoln, Abraham: *Complete Works of Abraham Lincoln,* edited by John G. Nicolay and John Hay. New York, Frances T. Tandy Company, 1905.

Milton, George Ford: *The Eve of Conflict: Stephen A. Douglas and the Needless War.* Boston and New York, Houghton Mifflin Company, 1934.

Randall, Ruth Painter: *Mary Lincoln, Biography of a Marriage.* Boston, Little Brown and Company, 1953.

Sandburg, Carl: *Abraham Lincoln, the Prairie Years.* New York, Harcourt, Brace and Company, 1926.

Shehean, James W.: *The Life of Stephen Arnold Douglas.* New York, Harper and Brothers, 1860.

Also

Bowers, Claude G.: "Lincoln and Douglas." Springfield, Illinois, *Abraham Lincoln Association Papers,* 1930.

Douglas, Stephen A.: "Autobiography." Springfield, Illinois, *Journal of the Illinois State Historical Society,* Vol. V, October, 1921.

Goodspeed, Thomas Wakefield: "Lincoln and Douglas." Springfield, Illinois, *Journal of the Illinois State Historical Society,* Vol. XXVI, April-January, 1933-34.

Hodder, Frank Heywood: "Railroad Background of the Kansas-Nebraska Act." *Mississippi Valley Historical Review,* Vol. XII, June-March, 1925-26.

Lynch, William O.: "The Character and Leadership of Stephen A. Douglas." *Mississippi Valley Historical Review,* March, 1923.

Salisbury, Herbert Spencer: "The Mormon War in Hancock County." Springfield, Illinois. *Journal of the Illinois State Historical Society,* Vol. VIII, April-January, 1915-16.

Stevens, Frank E.: "Life of Stephen Arnold Douglas." Springfield, Illinois. *Journal of the Illinois State Historical Society,* Vol. XVI, October-January, 1923-24.

*Dictionary of American Biography.* New York, Charles Scribner's Sons, 1936.

*Encyclopedia of American History,* edited by Richard M. Morris. New York, Harper and Brothers, 1953.

*Encyclopaedia Britannica.*

Also

"Stephen Arnold Douglas, Chicagoan and Patriot." An address delivered at the Chicago Historical Society, June 2, 1961, by Paul M. Angle.

# INDEX

187

## About the Author

JEANNETTE COVERT NOLAN was
born in Indiana and has lived there all her
life. Her forebears came to the Hoosier
state as pioneers, and her grandfather was
one of its first newspaper editors. On
graduation from high school, she worked
as a reporter and feature writer on newspapers in Evansville until she married. As
her three children were growing up, she
turned seriously to writing books, the
first of which was published in 1932.
Since then she has written many books of
fiction and biography, also short stories,
plays and essays. She has taught creative
writing at Indiana University and served
as a staff member at five Writers' Conferences there; twice she conducted juvenile workshops at the University of
Colorado Writers' Conference. Several of
her books have been selections of the
Junior Literary Guild, and she has twice
been the winner of the Indiana University Award for the "Most Distinguished
Juvenile Book by an Indiana Author."